Pat Baker

The Joint Board of Christian Education
Melbourne

Published by
The Joint Board of Christian Education
Second Floor, 10 Queen Street, Melbourne 3000, Australia

SIMULATION GAMES 4

National Library of Australia
  Cataloguing-in-Publication entry

Baker, Patricia, 1932-
  Simulation games 4.

ISBN 0 85819 802 9.

1. Games in Christian education. 2. Simulation games in education. I. Joint Board of Christian Education. II. Title.

268.6

First printed 1991

Cover and illustrations: Stephen Stanley
Design: Pat Baker
Typeset: JBCE in Bitstream Swiss on Ventura Publisher
Printer: Globe Press Pty Ltd
JB91/2964

Contents

Introducing Simulation Games 4 –
When you're on a good thing...

I can't believe that it's almost five years since *Simulation Games 3* made its appearance! But it is – and at last comes the next in the series, with nineteen more games.

The catalyst for this volume arrived on my desk about a year ago in the form of a letter from Darryl Grafton in Columbus, Ohio, asking if we would be interested in seeing some games he had developed. Subsequently Darryl sent "Nuclear Negotiations" and another game and *Simulation Games 4* was under way. While seeking permission to use "The Carpenter from Nazareth" I wrote to Harry Burgraaf, a member of the *Hezekiah* editorial panel. Along with his reply came the offer of "Spread the Flame!" And when I asked Geoff Hunter for permission to use his "Strategy for Mission" he suggested some improvements to the original version.

That kind of personal contact with game-makers is always good. Earlier, Daniel McDiarmid had sent "Radiola Church" along with the manuscript of a book he was writing about stewardship. At that stage there were no immediate plans for *Simulation Games 4*, but we were able to use his game in *On the Move*.

One of the problems with trying to finalise material for this book and its predecessor has been tracing copyright holders for games that have been published previously. It is not difficult when they have been handled by major publishing houses, but a number of the games in our files first appeared in small and long defunct periodicals. "Great Minds" in *Simulation Games 3* was modelled on a game by Kathy Brophy Frick which was written up in one of these periodicals. When I looked at "Make policy, not coffee" from the same author and same source, I noticed that Kathy Brophy Frick was identified as a doctoral student. With the help of the Alumni Association of Indiana University, I was able to get in touch with Kathy and received her permission to reproduce "Make policy" here.

Some games we would like to have included are not here – either because we were not able to trace the copyright holder, or because the reproduction fee was more than we could afford.

I don't know whether there will be a volume 5. That will depend on a number of factors. One is the continuing use of simulation games by teachers and youth and community workers. Another is the willingness of people creating games to share them with us and thus with others.

Pat Baker
November 1990

P.S. I assume that anyone who buys a book called *Simulation Games 4* will already be experienced in conducting simulations. The earlier volumes in the series included "how to" sections which are worth re-reading if you have them.

Summarising the games in this book

Here you can see at a glance what each game is about, how many players can take part, and how much time you will need.

The games are listed under headings that you may find helpful in locating a game for a specific use.

The Bible and church history

THE CARPENTER FROM NAZARETH

About: the person of Jesus and the effect he had on others
Number of players: at least 20
Time needed: $1\frac{1}{2}$ to 2 hours

IN THE TIME OF THE MACCABEES

About: the time between the Old and New Testaments
Number of players: 2 to 20
Time needed: about 30 minutes

JEWS AND GENTILES

About: cultural differences in the early church
Number of players: minimum of 10
Time needed: about 45 minutes

The church today

WHAT CAN WE SAVE?

About: what we value in the local church
Number of players: any number
Time needed: 30 minutes or more

FUTURE CHURCH

About: negotiating desirable futures for the church
Number of players: 12 to 36
Time needed: at least 2 hours

RADIOLA CHURCH

About: stewardship and Christian giving
Number of players: minimum of 10
Time needed: about 1 hour

STRATEGY FOR MISSION

About: designing a strategy for local church mission
Number of players: any number
Time needed: 3 hours

Christian living

THE DISCIPLESHIP GAME

About: being Christian
Number of players: up to 15
Time needed: about 1 hour

SPREAD THE FLAME!

About: being Christian
Number of players: 5 to 10
Time needed: 30 minutes or more

Priorities

CAVE-IN
About: survival and values
Number of players: 5 to 20
Time needed: about 1 hour

PROJECTS FOR A NEW WORLD
About: working for a better world
Number of players: minimum of 10
Time needed: about 1 hour

Family life

THE FAMILY GAME
About: roles and relationships in the family
Number of players: about 6
Time needed: about 1 hour

Women

MAKE POLICY, NOT COFFEE
About: status of women
Number of players: any number
Time needed: 1 to 2 hours

Interdependence and co-operation

A GLASS BEAD GAME
About: making connections
Number of players: any number
Time needed: flexible

MAKING AND IMPROVING
About: basic economic concepts
Number of players: any number
Time needed: 1 hour

TAMUSE
About: co-operation
Number of players: 8
Time needed: about 15 minutes

Cultural differences

CULTURE GAME
About: cultural misunderstandings
Number of players: any number
Time needed: 90 minutes

Power/violence/war

NUCLEAR NEGOTIATIONS
About: international tensions
Number of players: 6 to 24
Time needed: $1\sqrt{2}$ to 2 hours

THE STRUCTURAL VIOLENCE GAME
About: structural violence
Number of players: any number
Time needed: 30 minutes or more

The carpenter from Nazareth

A biblical simulation by Robert De Feyter

Purpose

The purpose of this simulation is to get a feel for New Testament times and to deepen your understanding of the person of Jesus.

Process

Each member of your group is allocated a particular New Testament group, e.g. Pharisee, Zealot, Trader etc. The number of each group will depend on the size of your group.

The game is played in three steps:

1. Each of the groups discover their identity and decide on the roles they will play – through the study of various New Testament passages and Bible reference material. (Time about 40-60 minutes.)

2. Role play the market place scene. Interact with each other according to the identity and roles assumed. Simulate as closely as possible a New Testament market place scene where people are discussing the person of Jesus of Nazareth.

3. A Grand Council in the Market Place called together by Herod to decide on the question "Who is this Jesus?" (teacher, rebel, Son of God, fanatic, leader etc.) where each of the groups present their case.

NOTE:

You can get Herod to call the Council and direct it, or the game director could do it as an impartial figure. Make sure everyone gets a fair go and the question is discussed seriously with each group giving biblically and historically based reasons. You can conclude with a democratic vote on the matter.

Preparation

1. You will need enough space for each of the groups to meet to study and discuss separately their roles. Also a central space to play out the market place scene.

2. It is best to inform individuals or groups beforehand what they will be so that they can bring along appropriate costumes, props, scenery etc., e.g. traders bring typical N.T. foodstuffs and wares to sell in the market place;
Pharisees dress like Pharisees;
the sick – use imagination to portray leprosy, amputation, malnutrition etc.

3. Use your imagination to set the scene as realistically as possible.

4. Have some reference books available (Bible dictionary, N.T. introduction, articles on Zealots etc.) as well as enough Bibles.

The game director gives the following instructions and monitors the time for each stage.

Reprinted from HEZEKIAH – Publication of Reformed Church Youth of Australia. Used by permission.

INSTRUCTIONS

(Hand out a copy to each group.)

THE SITUATION

The year is A.D. 29. You are in the town of Bethany, near Jerusalem. Bethany is a fair sized town of several thousand people, including scholars, craftsmen, priests, shepherds, traders and soldiers. In the centre of the town is the market place, a bustling hubbub of people. It is the setting for our simulation.

The whole of Judea is talking about this person "Jesus", called the Nazarene. Gossip is rife, rumours abound. Not many people really know who he is. Rumours and stories have filtered down from Galilee about many miracles and events occurring there. Apparently, huge crowds have been following him.

Now, Jesus is reported to be on his way toward Bethany and many people have converged there to try to see him. Everyone has flocked to the market place because that's where the action is. Everyone is arguing heatedly, debating, asking questions and trying to convince others of their own view.

You are

(a) to work out the identity of your group and the roles you will play,

(b) to simulate the gathering of the people in the market place, the controversy and arguing that is going on, and the interactions between the various groups of people.

(c) to contribute to a Grand Council to decide on the question "Who is this Jesus?"

PREPARATION AND RESEARCH
(40-60 minutes)

1. Appoint a leader of your group if one hasn't already been appointed. He or she should direct the members of the group in carrying out the group task.

2. Appoint a chronicler who will record the action of the simulation from the perspective of his or her particular group, and report to the debriefing session.

3. Each person should choose a biblical name for themselves (e.g. use Matthew 1 or Luke 3 as resources). Briefly, make up personal details about yourself such as age, family, town of birth, tribe of Israel ...

4. Examine any resource material supplied and establish the identity of your particular group, e.g. discuss what status your group of people had within Jewish society. What were your attitudes to the other groups?

5. As a group, using any texts as a basis, decide on what sort of opinions you will have about Jesus that are appropriate to your group. Be able to defend those opinions.

6. Discuss the task that your group has been given and how you can fulfill it. Discuss what type of questions you can ask other people, and of which groups, that will assist you in this. Allocate particular jobs within the group if necessary.

THE MARKET SCENE *(20-30 minutes)*

Go out into the market place, as directed by your leader, and try to fulfill your group's tasks. Use pen and paper to jot notes if necessary. In any situation or interaction that arises, act out your role. Comply with any directions from your group leader or from the game director.

THE GRAND COUNCIL *(15+ minutes)*

A meeting will be arranged of all the various factions and groups. Questions may be asked of your group. Decide who will represent your group at the council. Be prepared to respond as appropriate. The question at issue is "Who is this Jesus?"

DEBRIEFING

The simulation ought to be concluded with a time of debriefing.

Questions which might be discussed:

1. How did you feel about your role?

2. How realistic was the simulation?

3. How easy/difficult was it to come to an accurate understanding of your group identity – was it accurate?

4. Did it do justice to what the Bible says about Jesus?

5. In what way has your appreciation and understanding of New Testament times and Jesus developed?

SUMMARY OF GROUPS

Disciples

Followers of Jesus, chosen by him. Jesus had told them many parables and they had seen many miracles. They were the closest to him.

Pharisees

The religious leaders. Proud and aloof, protectors fo the Law. They looked for a Messiah or prophet, but were more interested in their traditions and in upholding the Law.

Herod and his court

King of the Jews. He ruled with the backing of the Romans, and was supported by the Pharisees. He wanted to prevent any disturbances and to protect his own position.

Zealots

This underground organisation aimed to overthrow the Roman occupying forces and re-establish a Jewish kingdom. They had a high regard for the Law.

Traders

Simple people who earned their living by selling goods in the market place. Renowned for their story-telling and rumour-mongering.

Tax collectors

Servants of the Romans, they often oppressed the people and so were hated by most. As outcasts, they stuck to themselves a lot.

John the Baptist

A prophet. He had a number of disciples and followers. He spoke out against the Pharisees and Herod, and was considered a radical by some.

Josephus

A Jewish historian. He compiled an extensive history of the period. As a historian, he was impartial and fair.

The sick

There were many diseased and maimed. Lepers were outcasts and could live only by begging.

P

DISCIPLES

Suggest you use the following: Simon (leader); Matthew; John; Luke (chronicler: Luke 1:1-4) – even though he wasn't a disciple.

Identity: Mark 1:14-20; 2:13-14; Matthew 10:1-20.

Background information: John 14:1-14; Matthew 1:29-34; 3:7-12; 9:33-37.

Who is Christ? Mark 8:27-30.

Tasks:
Jesus has sent you on ahead to Bethany, through which he is going to pass on his way to Jerusalem. He has asked you to do the following:

(a) Find out where you can get food and accommodation for several days in Bethany, for the whole group.

(b) Find out the mood of the people. What are people saying? You are to make a report to give to Jesus.

Be conscious of the need to protect Jesus and defend him. You already know the Jews want to kill him, so don't tell anyone where he is, only that he is coming.

Also, you must be able to defend Jesus
against accusations from the Pharisees: see Mark 2:23–3:6; 2:13-17; 7:1-15 (especially verse 15); John 7:21-24
against accusations from the Zealots: see Matthew 5:43-48.

JOHN THE BAPTIST AND DISCIPLES OF JOHN

Identity: Luke 1:5-25, 57-66, 80. Provide yourself with suitable clothing (blanket).

Attitudes and further information: Luke 3:1-20; 7:18-20; John 3:22-30; 1:19-28.

Tasks:
Rumour has it that Jesus is the Christ.

(a) Determine from the above texts what you think the Messiah would be and do.

(b) Send out your disciples to gather evidence, and decide whether you believe Jesus is the Christ.

Prepare a report on these two questions.

JOSEPHUS, THE JEWISH HISTORIAN

Identity: See resource books.
NOTE: You will have to pretend that you lived during Jesus' time.
You have two servants (scribes) to help you in your task.

Tasks:
(a) You are the official Jewish historian. You are to collect information for the next volume you are writing. The hottest topic around at the moment is Jesus of Nazareth. You suspect he may be worth a page or two. You may send out your two scribes to collect any information you can about Jesus, using a notebook.

(b) Don't be satisfied with rumours or hearsay. E.g. ask:
"Did you see him?"
"Were you there yourself?"
"What exactly did he do?"

(c) You must try to be impartial and scientific in your task. No decent historian tries to put his or her own interpretations or judgments on top of the facts, so stick to the facts. Try to determine what *really happened*. Try to speak to as many people as possible.

HEROD

Include in your group Herod, his wife, servants and Roman soldiers.

Identity: See resource books.

Attitudes: Mark 6:19-20.
To Jesus: your are perplexed (Luke 9:7-9).
To others: you are in command. You are ruler of the nation, and you take orders only from Caesar. You have under your command both soldiers and messengers.

Tasks:
(a) Caesar has heard about the civil unrest that has been occuring, particularly because of the Nazarene, Jesus. He wants a complete report: "Who is he? What is he doing?" etc. "Does he pay taxes to Caesar?"

(b) Determine whether Jesus is a potential political opponent. Is he claiming to be king? Why are people following him? You are worried by this possibility.

(c) It is your job to keep the peace and protect law and order. You have a squad of soldiers for that purpose. At the same time, you wish to be seen as impartial and fair and even-handed. Don't be influenced by factions.
Watch out particularly for those trouble-makers the Zealots. If they are causing any trouble, have them arrested. Likewise with John the Baptist. (NOTE: This simulation occurs before you have killed John the Baptist.)

PHARISEES

Leader: The High Priest.

Background information: See resource books.

Attitudes and opinions: Luke 18:9-14; Mark 7:1-8; 2:15-16; 2:23–3:6; John 11:45-53; 10:22-23.
Also, in relation to sick people, see Leviticus 13:1-11; 14:1-7.
Be able to describe how you will know the Christ: John 7:41-43.

Tasks:
(a) You are wary of this Jesus. He represents a threat to your position as religious leaders, since he is causing unrest and the people are following him. You wish to dispose of him, but of course this must be done properly and legally: within God's law. Hence you wish to bring him to trial, but you require witnesses and evidence to bring against him.

(b) Under orders of the High Priest (in Jerusalem), you must go out and collect evidence against Jesus, particularly eye-witness accounts. Try to find out where he is, when he is coming, where he will be staying. Locate any of his followers, so they may be watched.

(c) Your task is also to uphold the law of God: ensure that people observe the law.

(d) You may argue with anyone and try to convince anyone of your views about Christ, but remember that a Pharisee wouldn't even talk to some classes of people.

TRADERS

There are no special background texts to help establish your identity, so you will have to be creative in that. Look at the Gospels generally.

Attitude to Jesus: On the one hand, he could be good for business because he attracts large crowds, and many people come in from the countryside. On the other hand, you have heard of Jesus in Jerusalem (John 2:12-16).

Tasks:
(a) Set up stalls in the market place.
Suggestions: a blanket each, spread out on the ground. You can try to sell drinks, biscuits, bread, anything you can think of. (Make it realistic though.)

(b) Collect as many rumours and stories about Jesus as you can.

(c) Try to impress people by telling them stories that you have heard, even if you have to exaggerate.

TAX COLLECTORS

Identity: Matthew 9:9-13; 22:15-22; Luke 18:9-14.

Task:
You have received the enclosed letter:

Chief of Taxes
Head Office
Jerusalem

To the Regional Tax Office
Bethany

Greetings, in Caesar's name.

It has come to my notice that a certain Nazarene, Jesus by name, is encouraging people not to pay taxes. Such views must not be allowed to propogate among the people. I expect that this Jesus is one of those accursed outlaws, the Zealots.

Please report to me on the following:

(a) Who is this Jesus? Who do people say he is?

(b) What are his views on paying taxes?

(c) Does he pay allegiance to Caesar?

(d) What are his views on tax collectors? (I have heard rumours that he even associated with our lot, unlike other Jews.) Do you think he is a threat to our profession?

Report to me post haste
Simon Bar Manon
Chief of Taxes

P.S. You are to collect relevant information from people in the market place also.

THOSE WHO HAVE BEEN HEALED

Blind man: John 9.

Leper: Mark 1:40-45.

Tasks:
(a) Proclaim to anyone who will listen that you have been healed, how, by whom, etc.

(b) Decide whether you believe that Jesus is the Christ. Be able to defend your belief (yes or no).

THE SICK

Identity: Decide whether you want to be blind, lame, leper or anything else (demon possession?). Remember that lepers were outcasts: had to have a bell and call out "unclean".
Blind people would have to be led by others.
Lame people would have to be carried.

Regulations for lepers: Leviticus 13, 14.

Attitude of the sick in general: Mark 10:46-52.

Tasks:

(a) Decide whether you believe that Jesus can heal you. Why? For this you will have to collect evidence of previous healing miracles of Jesus. You must be able to demonstrate to people why you hold this belief.

(b) Try to find out where Jesus is, so that you may be healed.

ZEALOTS

Identity: See resource books.
Your group have a high regard for the law, and hate the Romans who you think are idolators. You look down on the Pharisees because they bow and scrape to the wishes of the Roman rulers, and Herod because he is a Roman puppet. Yours is a secret society, so don't tell anyone you are a Zealot.

Background:
Taxes: Luke 29:20-26
Worship: John 2:12-17
Revolution: Matthew 10:34-36
Also: Matthew 10:4; Isaiah 14:1-2; 34:1-2; Daniel 9:4-19.

Tasks:

(a) You must try to instigate a popular uprising against the Romans, and their puppet King Herod. To do this, you want to enlist the aid of the Nazarene miracle worker, Jesus, because many people follow him. He would be a great boost for your campaign.
Hence report to your leader on the questions:
Will Jesus support your plans?
Is he for or against the Romans?

(b) Determine what sort of person the Messiah, or Promised One, would be, according to your views.

Note: You hate the tax collectors and refuse to speak to them.

In the time of the Maccabees

A game about the time between the Old and New Testaments

Background

A tradition tells how the *dreidel* (DRY-dell), or top, came to be associated with Hanukkah. When Antiochus forbade the Jews to meet together to study the Scriptures or to worship, they met secretly and studied the Scriptures. Since most of the sacred books had been burned, they taught one another passages from memory. A lookout at the door would give the alarm if soldiers appeared, and the group would scatter. If they could not get away in time, they would begin to play with a *dreidel* that they always kept on a table in front of them. Thus, when the soldiers broke in, searching for Jews studying the forbidden Scriptures, they found instead a group of people playing an innocent game.

Today, dreidels are still used as a Hanukkah game. Each side of the dreidel contains a letter of the Hebrew alphabet: *nun* (N), *gimel* (G), *he* (H), and *shin* (SH).

The game

You will need:

A large copy of the game board; a dreidel; some kind of marker for each player; a set of dilemma cards, placed face down beside the board.

Procedure

1. Players represent Jews in the time of the Maccabees. The object of the game is to move from *Start* around the board until reaching the centre.

2. Players take it in turn to spin the dreidel. If *nun* faces up, move forward one space; if *gimel*, two spaces; *he*, three spaces; and *shin*, four spaces.

3. When a player lands on a space where instructions are written, these must be followed.

4. A player landing on a Star of David must take the top dilemma card, read it aloud, and then decide what action to take. The other players give the decision the "thumbs up" or "thumbs down" sign. If the "thumbs up" outnumber the "thumbs down", the player moves forward that number of spaces. If "thumbs down" are in the majority, the player moves back that number of spaces. In the case of a draw, the player does not move. If the vote is unanimous, the player moves forward or back five spaces.

5. The winner is the player (or team) reaching the centre first.

Reprinted from ADVENTURE, © Graded Press, The United Methodist Publishing House, Nashville. Used by permission.

NUN

GIMEL

SHIN   HE

DILEMMA CARDS

A

A Greek official is recruiting athletes for a big athletic competition. You want to participate, but the games are held on the sabbath.

- Yes, I will take part.
- No, I will not take part.

B

A sports arena, the centre of Greek social life, has been built in your town, and your friends are urging you to attend. The way of life encouraged at the arena goes against your religious beliefs.

- Yes, I will go to the arena.
- No, I will not go.

C

Many of your friends have changed their names to the Greek form to be more like their neighbours. You are proud of your Jewish name, but life would be easier for you if you changed your name.

- Yes, I will change my name.
- No, I won't change it.

D

The spread of Greek culture has caused business to boom.

- Yes, the advances under the Greeks are worth giving up some of our old ways.
- No, some of our beliefs are too important to give up for financial gain.

E

What difference does it make that we can't worship in the Temple?

- Yes, we can worship privately just as well.

- No, public worship together as God's family is important.

F

It is hard to do without our Bibles.

- Yes, but I know some Scripture passages by heart.

- No, I have not memorised any Scripture that would be helpful now that written Bibles are forbidden.

G

Fighting on the sabbath is against my religious beliefs.

- Yes, I will refuse to fight on the sabbath even if I die for it.

- No, I will fight to preserve the freedom to worship God, even on the sabbath.

H

Perhaps we are just stubborn in refusing to accept the Greek ways.

- Yes, people would be better off if they weren't so different.

- No, people have the right to worship God in their own way and to keep their own identity.

I

It doesn't matter if we can't celebrate our religious festivals.

- Yes, religion is more than festivals anyways.

- No, festivals are important ways to express our religious beliefs.

J

We probably will never face losing our religious freedom today.

- Yes, we are guaranteed religious freedom.

- No, we must carefully preserve our religious freedom.

A Hanukkah board game laid out on a grid of squares.

START		You wear Greek clothing; GO AHEAD 1 SPACE		Caught in the Temple on the Sabbath; GO BACK 2 SPACES	A (Star of David)
Greeks sacrifice pigs on the Temple altar; GO BACK 2 SPACES	E (Star of David)	Fresh supplies arrive; GO AHEAD 2 SPACES		Can't find fresh water; RETREAT 3 SPACES	
		Greek soldiers make a last ditch effort; GO BACK 3 SPACES	I (Star of David)		
		Caught reading your Bible; GO BACK TO START	(menorah)	F (Star of David)	Head for the hills to avoid pagan worship; GO AHEAD 4 SPACES
Greeks attack on Elephants; LOSE 1 TURN	You help cleanse the Temple; GO AHEAD 2 SPACES			Your family worshipS secretly on the Sabbath; GO AHEAD 2 SPACES	
	H (Star of David)		Not by might, nor by power, but by my Spirit, says the LORD of hosts.	You found oil for the Hanukka lights; GO AHEAD 4 SPACES	Greek soldiers destroy your Bible; LOSE 1 TURN
D (Star of David)	You go to the Greek gymnasium; GO BACK 5 SPACES	Celebrate the re-dedication of the Temple; GO AHEAD 1 SPACE			B (Star of David)
You changed your name to a Greek form; GO AHEAD 2 SPACES			J (Star of David)	You recover the lampstand; GO AHEAD 2 SPACES	
		You hide some of the Maccabees; GO AHEAD 3 SPACES	G (Star of David)	Caught calling Antiochus "The Madman"; GO BACK TO START	Successful raid on Greek soldiers; GO AHEAD 3 SPACES
You teach your friends Bible verses from memory; GO AHEAD 4 SPACES		Your raiders ambushed; GO BACK 1 SPACE	C (Star of David)		Caught saying your prayers; GO BACK 2 SPACES

P

19

Jews and Gentiles

A role-playing game for any number of players, adapted from a game by E. Jane Mall

Purpose

To illustrate the problems Paul faced in trying to reconcile Christians from Jewish and Gentile backgrounds, and to relate these to differences among Christians today.

Background

Paul seems to have spent much of his Christian life struggling with the forces of Judaism. Even within the church there was constant tension between Jews who had accepted the gospel and people who had come to Christ from outside the Jewish tradition. If Gentiles were to become Christians, these Jewish believers said, they must first accept the disciplines of the Jewish faith: they must be circumcised and observe the Law. But to Paul and some others it was becoming increasingly clear that Christianity was not just an offshoot of Judaism but God's new beginning for all humankind. As such, it could not accept the restrictions of the Law.

Paul and the Jerusalem leaders hammered out their differences in the meeting described in Acts 15:1-29. Paul, in his writings as well as in his preaching, continued to stress the universal nature of the gospel. See Galatians, especially 3:26-29, and Romans 10:9-13 and 1 Corinthians 12:12-13.

The situation

In the game we imagine that Paul has set up a situation to help the rival Christian groups examine their differences and, hopefully, to help them to a fuller understanding of the essentials of the Christian faith.

Members of the two groups will have the chance to "buy" what they believe is essential for the church.

Roles

There are two individual roles and two group roles. The individuals are PAUL (who should be played by a leader) and a BEGGAR (whose role is not revealed to the other players). The groups are the JEWISH CHRISTIANS and the GENTILE CHRISTIANS

Preparation

1. Set up a table with symbolic items on it. Each item bears a label, showing what it represents. Each item also has a concealed price tag. (You may use real or play money, whichever is more convenient, and price the items accordingly.)

badge	tradition – high price
banner	freedom – low price
bread	Lord's Supper – low price
cross	salvation by faith – low price
key	exclusiveness – high price
knife	circumcision – high price
knotted cord	community – low price
piece of fruit	food laws – high price
prayer book	prayer – low price
ruler	equality – low price
scroll	the Law – high price
water	baptism – low price
whistle	discipline – high price

2. Total the amounts on the price tags and add about 10%. Halve that total to get the amount each group will have to trade with.

3. Prepare the role descriptions (see page xx) and money for distribution to participants.

Playing the game

1. After setting aside PAUL and the BEGGAR (whose roles are not revealed), divide the remaining players into two equal groups: JEWISH CHRISTIANS and GENTILE

CHRISTIANS. Give out the role descriptions and money.

2. Explain the action of the game: Paul (who may be introduced at this point) has set up a situation to help the Jewish and Gentile Christians examine their differences. The members of each group may "buy" from the table the items they want most for the church. They must not look at the price tags. They should select and buy those items which are important to their group, taking into account their role description. Stress that the items should be chosen for what they represent, rather than for what they actually are. Five minutes will be allowed for players to study their roles and decide strategy. After that there will be a short speech by Paul, followed by a 10-minute trading period. The game director will act as "shopkeeper". Players may take turns, argue, bargain etc. Answer questions for clarification.

3. The players study role descriptions and decide strategy. After 5 minutes call on Paul to make a speech.

4. Paul makes his speech, then announces the beginning of the trading period.

5. Five minutes after the trading period begins, the beggar comes in. He/she pleads for help, charity, appeals to the love and compassion of both groups. They respond as they see fit.

6. Call time at the end of the 10-minute trading period.

7. Ask the players to sit down together, mixing up the groups. Discuss what happened in the game:

- What items were bought by each group? Why? How much money did they have left? Were they able to buy all they wanted?

- Did anyone take any notice of Paul's speech?

- What happened to the beggar? How did the other players feel about him/her?

- Was either group more "Christian" than the other? In what way?

- Are there similar differences among Christians today?

- Which of the items offered would you want to "buy" for the church today? What else would you want?

- Could two such different groups ever work together on anything? Should they? If they did work together, would it be better for each group to retain its own ideas and principles or should they merge completely?

First published in the NEW BEGINNINGS GAMES PACKET (JBCE)

21

JEWISH CHRISTIANS

You are bound by Jewish law and traditions. You regard circumcision as essential and are careful about the observance of food laws. You disapprove of the Gentile Christians who often eat unclean food, refuse to be circumcised, are sometimes immoral, and generally disregard the Law. You do not willingly mix with Gentiles, whether they are Christians or not. You are well disciplined and make decisions as a group.

During the game you must observe these rules:

1) You must tithe – 10% of your income must be set aside for the Temple.

2) All decisions must be made by the group.

3) You must uphold your precious Law and traditions.

GENTILE CHRISTIANS

You are a new group with no traditions behind you. You are not even very much of a group: you are unorganised and very free and flexible. Your members are used to acting independently and don't care much for discipline. You are free to interpret the Christian faith as you will. All that binds you together is a common faith in Jesus Christ.

Guidelines for the game:

1) You are free to act as you choose.

2) Decisions may be made together or independently.

PAUL

You have called the rival groups of Jewish and Gentile Christians together to examine their differences and, hopefully, to help them to a fuller understanding of the essentials of the Christian faith. You will be expected to make an opening speech, urging the two groups to overcome their differences and accept each other as brothers and sisters in Christ. (You could quote Galatians 3:26-29; Romans 10:9-13; 1 Corinthians 12:12-13.)

BEGGAR

You come into the game half-way through the trading period. The other players are un-aware of your identity. You are in urgent need of money. (You may make up any story you like.) Approach members of both groups for help.) Be insistent. Appeal to their love and compassion as Christians. Remind them of Jesus' parable in Matthew 25:31-46.

What can we save?

A game by Pat Baker about what we value in the local church

Purpose

To make group decisions about what is of greatest value in our local church.

Materials needed

Statement of task, large sheet of paper and felt pen for each group of 4-5 people.

Players

Any number of people can participate in groups of 4-5. The optimum number is 20-30.

Scenario

Imagine some future time when Christianity has been outlawed. The ruling powers have decreed that all churches and their contents will be destroyed and all known Christians executed or imprisoned. You have gathered in your local church to seek God's guidance. A messenger arrives, breathless and afraid. A detachment of storm troopers is just down the road and heading in this direction. You have roughly 10 minutes in which to save what you can and head for the hills.

Process

1. Form groups of 4-5 people.

2. Outline the scenario.

3. Give each group a copy of the task statement, a large sheet of paper and a felt pen.

4. Say that the groups have 10 minutes in which to complete their task. You will give warnings after 8 and 9 minutes.

5. At the end of 10 minutes, call the groups together.

6. Have the groups display their lists.

7. Debrief and discuss.

YOUR TASK

Ten minutes from now your church building will be destroyed. You must save what you can and head for a safe hiding place in the hills.

You can save just 10 items. For the purposes of the game, size and weight are of no significance. As a group you must decide what things are most necessary and of most value to maintain the church underground.

Only those items listed on your sheet of paper at the end of 10 minutes will be saved.

Questions for discussion

1. What items were common to all lists?

2. What items were common to some but not all lists?

3. What items were chosen by one group only?

4. How were decisions reached in your group?

5. Were you satisfied with the group's choices?

6. What were your reasons for choosing the items you chose?

Future church

A game about negotiating desirable futures by Pat Baker

Purpose

For participants to explore their hopes for the church by negotiating possible future trends.

Number of players: 12-36

Time needed: 2 hours minimum

Materials

A copy of the FUTURE CHURCH statements and a pen or pencil for each participant, a supply of newsprint and felt-tipped pens for Rounds Two and Three.

Process

Explain that participants will receive a list of statements about what the church may possibly be like in the future. The game will be played in three rounds. In Round One everyone will work alone, ranking the *desirability* of every statement by numbering it 1 to 7 (1 = highly undesirable; 7 = highly desirable). In Rounds Two and Three they will negotiate with other participants.

ROUND ONE

Hand out the FUTURE CHURCH statements. Stress that there is to be no interaction between participants. Each person must work alone at ranking the desirability of each future possibility. Approximately 30 minutes will be allowed for this round.

(In most cases 30 minutes is long enough for this round, but aim to be flexible and allow a little more time if participants seem to need it.)

ROUND TWO

Ask participants to form "task teams" (groups) of three or four people. Suggest that they team with people whom they don't know well. (This is designed to minimise the grouping of like with like.)

Instruct the task teams to *negotiate* a consensus list of 15 most desirable futures from the original list. Make clear the ground rules for consensus: no voting, no trading, no appointing a leader, no resorting to power or strong arm tactics. Task team members must *persuade* rather than push each

other around. Say that they will have 45 minutes in which to choose and list their 15 most desirable futures.

The game director should casually circulate among the task teams as they negotiate to assure that the negotiating consensus-seeking process doesn't break down into more traditional power-oriented modes of decision making.

Warn the task teams after 40 minutes that their list should be nearing completion. (Allow extra time if necessary.) The task teams display their lists where everyone can see them.

ROUND THREE

The final round involves negotiating a total group consensus of the 15 most desirable futures from among the task team lists. The ground rules are the same as for Round Two: decision must be by consensus. Say that they have 30 minutes in which to come up with the consensus listing.

Do not tell them how to organise themselves for this round. (One of the silent agendas of the game is "group process". There is a complimentarity between the open and experimental nature of the future itself, and the open and experimental method of negotiating desirable futures through participatory and "democratic" activities.)

Debriefing

There should be a period of debriefing and discussion. Start with some general questions, e.g.

- What happened?
- What did you experience?
- How did you feel about it?

You may want to go on to more specific discussion of the final consensus statements, e.g.

- Is this the kind of church you would like to be part of in twenty years' time?
- Where does the church seem to be heading?
- What part do we have in its future?
- What can we do now to work toward a desirable future for the church?

Future Church is based on the Hybrid Delphi Game by Jerome R. Saroff, described in SIMULATION/ GAMING/NEWS, November 1975.

FUTURE CHURCH

Can you imagine what the church might be like twenty years from now? Listed here are a number of possible future trends. It is your task to rank each one according to how desirable or undesirable you consider it to be. Place a number from 1 to 7 in the box beside each statement:

1 = highly undesirable (over your dead body!).

7 = highly desirable (that's the kind of future church you'd like to be part of).

General

☐ The church will be pretty much as we know it today.

☐ The church will be illegal and will have to go underground.

☐ No one will really care whether the church exists or not.

Organisation

☐ There will be no heirarchical structures.

☐ Local churches will be increasingly autonomous.

☐ Our denomination will have combined/united with three other denominations.

☐ The trend will be towards non-denominational "super-churches" with a membership of at least 500.

☐ Social justice activists will form their own church.

☐ House churches will outnumber conventional congregations.

☐ Church services will be replaced by community service throughout the week.

☐ Worship services will be monthly, with weekly meetings for support action and study being in small groups.

☐ All church activities (including committees, clubs and organisations) will take place on Sunday.

Leadership

☐ All major denominations will have bishops.

☐ The majority of clergy will be female.

☐ The pope will be a woman.

☐ All clergy will be male.

☐ Ministers and priests will take second jobs to pay expenses.

☐ Many clergy will be replaced by lay leaders.

☐ There will be no clergy.

☐ A clergy union will be established.

☐ All ministers will have to be single.

☐ It will be compulsory for all ministers to be married.

☐ Most congregations will have a volunteer and part-time staff team including youth worker, evangelist and pastoral visitor.

☐ Each local church will employ a business administrator.

Property

☐ The church will own no property.

- [ ] Most congregational buildings will have been sold to provide for larger regional church centres catering flexibly for 6-10 congregations.

- [ ] Church buildings will be open daily.

- [ ] Traditional church buildings will be replaced by worship centres with facilities for all ages to worship concurrently.

- [ ] Church buildings will be sold to provide funds for the poor.

- [ ] Churches will be located in shopping centres and open during shopping hours.

- [ ] Many churches will be located in shopping malls.

- [ ] Small chapels open all the time will replace churches that open only on Sundays.

- [ ] All church buildings will be so designed that they may be used every day of the week.

- [ ] Many churches will install Christian poker machines (i.e.with religious symbols) on their premises.

- [ ] Church buildings will be increasingly used for sanctuary by political refugees.

Membership

- [ ] There will be no women left in the church.

- [ ] Women will outnumber men in the congregations by three to one.

- [ ] Men will outnumber women in the congregations by three to one.

- [ ] There will be roughly equal numbers of men and women in most congregations.

- [ ] Church membership will be by subscription: an initial joining fee plus an annual fee.

- [ ] Church rolls will be culled annually. Anyone not attending on at least four Sundays during the year will have their membership cancelled.

- [ ] People under 30 will outnumber people over 30 in most congregations.

- [ ] All new members will be "on probation" and will be required to attend classes for their first two years.

Finance

- [ ] Big business will sponsor churches.

- [ ] The old practice of "pew rental" will be revived, i.e. people will pay an annual subscription for their own reserved seat in church.

- [ ] You will need to pay for admission to worship services, except for the first four pews.

- [ ] Women's organisations will raise most of the money for the upkeep of the local church.

- [ ] All churches will have facilities for credit cards.

- [ ] Government subsidies will be available to churches according to membership numbers.

- [ ] Most church finance will come from bequests.

- [ ] Church "collection" will be payable through a payroll debit system.

Worship

- [ ] Weeknight worship services will be almost as common as Sunday services.

- [ ] A central computer bureau will provide subscribers with ready-to-run Sunday services.

- [ ] Most ministers will get their Sunday sermons from a computer bulletin board.
- [ ] The Sunday sermon will be replaced by televised presentations by specialist preachers and teachers.
- [ ] Church "muzak" will replace live musicians.
- [ ] Synthesizers will replace organ music.
- [ ] Every church will have its own rock group for worship services.
- [ ] Scripture choruses will be the main form of church music.
- [ ] Worship services will use some of the best and most inspiring music in the world through CD discs.
- [ ] Most Sunday morning worship will be at 8.00 or 9.00 a.m., leaving the rest of the day free for other activities.
- [ ] Translations into many languages will be provided at all worship services.
- [ ] Sermons won't last more than 10 minutes. After that time, preachers have one minute warning and then pulpits self-destruct.
- [ ] Churches will be holy places where people are not allowed to chatter before or after services. Shoes must be removed at the door.
- [ ] Dancing will be part of worship at most services, with everyone participating.
- [ ] Church services will be held in nuclear shelters.

Education

- [ ] There will be a resurgence of the Sunday school.
- [ ] Sunday school teachers will be paid.
- [ ] Christian education will take place at home rather than in a Sunday school.
- [ ] Most Christian education programs will be available on videotape and computer disk.
- [ ] Fathers will line up for the privilege of teaching Sunday school.
- [ ] Adult study leaders will be able to order the latest study resources on particular topics each week by fax.
- [ ] Weekly Bible studies will be held through telephone link-ups, each member remaining in his/her own home. Much discussion will go into how to continue the tradition of "supper" when following this model.

Pastoral care

- [ ] "Shut-ins" will be able to play the videotape of last Sunday's service in their local church.
- [ ] "Easychurch" cards will give access to prayers and counselling 24 hours a day.
- [ ] Visiting needs will be computerised and prioritised.

Outreach

- [ ] All churches will have representatives on local councils.
- [ ] Chaplains will be on roster at all major shopping centres.
- [ ] There will be a national Christian daily newspaper.
- [ ] It will be illegal to speak in public places and the media about Christianity – considered an invasion of others' rights.
- [ ] One of the top League football teams will consist entirely of committed Christians.

P

☐ Mission projects, youth work and social justice projects will be the top three priorities of church budgets.

☐ Churches will advertise at sporting venues.

☐ A central computer bureau will provide weekly news bulletins for churches.

☐ Exchanges with overseas churches will be a common occurrence.

☐ Work will have started on a Third Testament supplement to the Bible.

☐ Christ will be recognised only as a prophet without divinity.

Radiola Church

A game about Christian giving by Daniel McDiarmid

The aims

The aims of this game are:
1. To show the various attitudes people have about giving money to the church.
2. To observe the processes by which a church can solve a financial dilemma.

The setting

Radiola Church is a simulation game for ten people. Form as many groups of ten as possible. Each group has eight characters seated around a table and two observers who can sit or stand behind the characters. Spare people can act as additional observers. Observers may read the participants' character descriptions. Each group has separate observers.

Allow 5 minutes for the introduction, 20 minutes for playing, and 20 minutes for the treasurer's report and discussion. If several groups are playing this last section may need longer time.

NOTES FOR THE GAME DIRECTOR

The aim of a simulation game is to reduce complex realities to manageable proportions. A real life situation is simplified and condensed so that the real forces involved in the more complex situation can be identified.

Do not presume that your group is familiar with simulation games. It is important to explain that this is a game of "Let's Pretend". Participants are asked to adopt the character of the person in their character description. Be warned that people who put too much of themselves into the character may end up revealing more about themselves thatn they otherwise would.

Remember too that you are embarking on a game. Like other games, this one has goals to be achieved and rules to be observed.

Introduction

Allocate the gamesheets to the participants. Each gamesheet contains the game description and a character description. Give the church treasurer's gamesheet and the minister's gamesheet to particular people. (Make sure they are not given to the real treasurer or minister of your church.) The treasurer should be a person who can keep order within the group for the duration of the playing time. Other gamesheets should be distributed randomly. The treasurer and observers will need pen and paper.

Read aloud the description. (Each person has a copy on their gamesheet.)

Playing time

Do not interfere with the groups, but observe the suggestions made by various people and the strategy employed by the group. After 18 minutes announce that there is only 2 minutes until the treasurer will be asked to report on the church's decision.

Treasurer's report and discussion

If several groups are playing, bring everyone back to their normal seating arrangements and ask each treasurer to report in turn. It is important to de-role people before the discussion begins. A simple exercise is to ask participants to stand up, walk once around the table and to sit down, no longer as their character, but as themselves again. At this point people may share their character descriptions if they wish.

After the treasurer's report ask the observers what attitudes about giving they detected among the participants and what they thought about the way the group accomplished its task.

You can lead the discussion with questions such as:

Did you feel that the character you were playing agreed with the decision made by the group?

Did your character feel challenged or pressured by anything that was said by others in the group?

(If several groups) Why did the different groups reach different conclusions?

What attitudes seen in the game are also apparent in our church?

What does the game teach us about raising money for our own church's activities?

First published in ON THE MOVE Issue 63 January 1989 (JBCE).

RADIOLA CHURCH

GAME DESCRIPTION

Radiola Church consists of the minister, the church treasurer, and six others. Each person receives an income and each person already gives money to the church. The local currency is rubels. Incomes vary from 100 rubels per week to 1,000 rubels per week.

Radiola Church has a "spare" church building (St Swineburn's) which could be sold, but church headquarters would not allow more than 5,200 rubels per year (100 rubels per week) to be used towards the local church budget.

The church's present income is 150 rubels per week. The church requires 300 rubels per week to carry on its present activities, but if it had an income of 350 rubels per week it could launch a really effective youth ministry.

The church treasurer has called a meeting of the entire church to find a way through this dilemma.

You have 20 minutes to prepare a plan to finance your church. The person whose gamesheet is marked "church treasurer" is the leader of the meeting and will be asked to report on how the Radiola Church is going to meet its budget.

Do not show your character description to any other character. (It may be shown to observers.) Other characters should only learn as much about you as you choose to reveal. Now read your character description. At the start of play the church treasurer and minister should make themselves known.

CHARACTER DESCRIPTION – the church treasurer

The bank manager has informed you that he has great concern about the Radiola Church's financial position.

You desperately need to solve the financial crisis.

Here are some of the options you might put to the group:
1. Ask each person to increase their giving by 20 rubels per week.
2. Charge an annual membership fee of, say, 2080 rubels per year (equivalent to 40 rubels per week).
3. Sell St Swineburn's and run fetes, street stalls etc.
4. Suggest each person gives a fixed proportion of their income. (Try various proportions, e.g. one percent, one tenth, one third etc.)
5. A combination of the above.

Personally you could probably give a bit more to the church if you wanted to.

Your income:	600 rubels per week
Your present giving:	40 rubels per week

32

CHARACTER DESCRIPTION – the minister

You are the minister of Radiola Church. You are embarrassed that the church is having a meeting to discuss giving because your wages are paid by the church.
On the other hand, you think it is important for people to develop a generous spirit and you encourage people to give money to the church. You believe that people should give a *proportion* of their income to the church.
Because of your family commitments you would find it very difficult to increase your giving by more than 5 rubels per week.

Your income: 400 rubels per week
Your present giving: 40 rubels per week

CHARACTER DESCRIPTION

You are a member of St Swineburn's Church. Your grandfather, a founding member of that church, is buried in the church grounds. You are strongly opposed to the proposal to sell this church.
You think everyone should pray more and the church finances will sort themselves out. You could give a lot more if convinced of the need.

Your income: 400 rubels per week
Your present giving: 5 rubels per week

CHARACTER DESCRIPTION

You are on a fixed income and already give every rubel you can possibly afford. You live very simply and cannot afford to give any more.
The principles of tithing, and the story of the widow's mite, are very important to you.

Your income: 100 rubels per week
Your present giving: 15 rubels per week

CHARACTER DESCRIPTION

You are a fairly easy-going person, one who follows the crowd, but you are suspicious of the church treasurer's attempts to organise giving within the Radiola Church. (You feel that money, like sex and politics, should not be talked about in public.)
You feel you could organise a monthly street stall which would raise 1250 rubels per year, equivalent to 25 rubels per week.

Your income: 300 rubels per week
Your present giving: 15 rubels per week

33

CHARACTER DESCRIPTION

Your spouse is not involved in the church. The income and giving figures below refer to your own money.
You are willing to increase your giving if asked (perhaps to 15 rubels per week) but you would rather organise an annual fete which would raise 2080 rubels, equivalent to 40 rubels per week.

Your income: 200 rubels per week
Your present giving: 10 rubels per week

(You also give 5 rubels per week to the *Let's Hear It For Hunger* campaign and regard this as part of your Christian giving.)

CHARACTER DESCRIPTION

You are employed in a very good job and keenly involved in the life of the church. Your four children are at that very expensive stage (lasting from birth to 25 years of age) but you could give more if convinced of the need.
You are often away on weekends and only give to the church when you are there. However you would like to see the Radiola Church have enough money to commence a really effective youth ministry. (Your own children could become involved.)

Your income: 800 rubels per week
Your present giving: 40 rubels
(about every second week)

CHARACTER DESCRIPTION

You are a person of great authority in the church. You like to hear your own voice and you like others to hear it too. You are the wealthiest member of the church. You don't give much to the church each week but regard yourself as very generous when special appeals are made.
If convinced of the need you could afford to give substantial amounts each week (100 rubels or more).

Your income: 1,000 rubels per week
Your present giving: 20 rubels per week

34

Strategy for mission

A simulation about designing an alternative strategy for local church mission by Geoff Hunter

The background

The Middleview Parish of the UCA (Uniting Church in Australia) is located in Yoretown, a city of around 100,000 people. In the years following World War II the centre of population moved to the northern side of Yoretown. In more recent times there has been a large expansion to the west.

The Middleview Parish is one of three UCA parishes in Yoretown. It comprises of three churches, each of which has a Sunday morning worship service. Central and North both have Sunday schools, and there is a small but active Parish youth group.

Central Church, five blocks south of the commercial centre of Yoretown, is a former Methodist Church, built just over 100 years ago. The church building is in need of expensive major repairs, though the Sunday school hall and rooms are in good condition. The congregation has been steadily decreasing in numbers over the past twenty years, even though several families who have moved west still come into Central to worship. New blocks of flats have sprung up on the city side, but the people living there don't seem interested in the church. The parish youth fellowship meets here every week.

North Church was also Methodist, and was established just after World War II as the town expanded into a city. The buildings are in excellent condition, but there is still a heavy debt. It has by far the best attendance of the three churches. Most members of the congregation are in their forties and fifties and include a number of professional people.

East Church was formerly Presbyterian. It was built 90 years ago and is badly in need of repair. Membership has declined to a few older life-long residents. East is located in what was once the residential hub of Yoretown (prior to the burgeoning of the northern area). The neighbourhood has a rapidly changing population, the latest of whom are of Indo-chinese origin. Old houses are being converted into flats, and there are a lot of social problems.

The scenario

You face the situation that there will **not** be a minister available for Middleview Parish next year.

Your Presbytery has a Strategy Committee which is suggesting that the Presbytery may have to adopt a wider sharing of the available ministers within the Presbytery.

Your Parish Council is due to meet again in two months to consider what action the parish is to take.

Two weeks ago, you were appointed to a special parish committee whose task it is to consider an alternative strategy to the present situation for your parish.

Last week the committee met, appointed a chair-person and secretary, and three sub-committees were formed in order to help speed up the planning process. You have less than two months before you have to report to the Parish Council.

Time

For this simulation game a period of 15 minutes = 4 hours meeting time. A three minute warning will be given prior to the end of each (15 minute) session, at which time you should summarise the meeting and formally adjourn. During the two minute break, you are to stand up, move around, and then resume a **different** seat in your group. (This will simulate the week's break between meetings.)

A note to the facilitator:

This simulation uses Uniting Church terminology. There is no reason why it should not work effectively with participants of a different denomination – but you will need to revise the scenario and make appropriate changes in the material for the various task forces.

There are a couple of other things you will need to keep in mind.

1. The simulation is pressurised in time. Its objective is not to get a new strategy out of the simulation itself, but to expose the participants to the possibilities of lateral thinking. Steps 4 and 8 could have extended time if available.

2. The most important phase is the debriefing time. If anything, one should err on more time in Step 10.

Questions that may be addressed during debriefing and subsequent discussion:

A. Assessing the conclusions
    – What are the "traditional" approaches that have been incorporated?
    – What innovations have been considered?

    – What constraints prevented innovative thinking?
    – What conflicts of interests were apparent?
    – What were the road blocks?
B. Discussion on a future strategy for your own mission task
    – What are the similarities to your situation?
    – What would you now be seeking to do?
    – Of what would you be wary?

Process

1. Introduction to the game. *(10 minutes)*
2. Divide into groups and read the materials. *(10 minutes)*
3. **2nd Week:** Task – to **define the mission** of the church. In the three sub-committees choose a definition, using the given list or adding your own definitions. *(10 minutes)*
4. Return to the full committee to resolve the definition to be used in this task. *(10 minutes)*
5. **3rd Week:** (Sub-committees)
    During the preceeding two weeks two members of each sub-committee have met independently to make up a list of factors which may be considered.
    The lists of each have been circulated to other sub-committees.
    You are to investigate initially the list for your sub-committee, using the check list and then if there is time "dream" or "brainstorm" other likely factors. *(15 minutes)*
6. **4th Week:** (Sub-committees)
    Continue work on the list of factors, choosing at this meeting those recommendations you would make to the total committee next week. *(15 minutes)*
7. **5th Week:** (Full committee)
    Review the work of the sub-committees. *(15 minutes)*
8. **6th Week:** (Full committee)
    Complete your report to Parish Council, listing the recommendations for an alternative strategy for your parish. *(15 minutes)*
9. **7th Week:** (Parish Council)
    The secretary of the strategy committee reports to the Parish Council. *(10 minutes)*
10. "Debrief" from the game and participate in general discussion on future strategy for our own mission task. *(60 minutes +)*

THE PURPOSE OF THE CHURCH ?

some views

1. To prepare the children and youth for membership in the church.

2. To teach the Bible.

3. To perform weddings, funerals, baptisms, give to the poor, and to provide Sunday school and youth groups.

4. To be the instrument of security and stability for the moral welfare of the community.

5. To find out what Christ is doing and to do it with him.

6. To prevent the spread of communism.

7. To help us solve our problems.

8. To enable people both to develop understandings of the gospel of Jesus Christ, and to live according to those implications of the gospel for daily life.

9. To declare the victory of Christ in such a way that men and women come into commitment to him, and that the community may be judged and renewed.

10. To express God's love to the world.

11. To provide opportunity for people to worship God.

12. To be God's people by participating in God's activities.

13.

14.

P

TASK FORCE ONE

1. The Synod paper reports on a lay administrator who had been used successfully in another parish to relieve the minister of most of the administrative tasks.

2. A team ministry has been suggested by Mr Hume and Mrs Smith who came recently from another Synod where "joint parishes" are operating with some success. They raise the question as to whether we could share the ministerial resources of the Presbytery jointly, i.e. across the present parish boundaries.

3. In a recent Presbytery meeting, the Rev. Howard Brown of the nearby city parish reports having made a number of pastoral visits to his people within the boundaries of your parish and further west.

4. The Rev. Laura Dunn, in a nearby parish, has successfully developed some small groups which meet fortnightly in private homes. This seems to provide excellent pastoral care for its members, relieving the minister of some of those immediate responsbilities.

5. Your regional Christian education officer is looking for a church willing to experiment in a "whole family" worship and study program as an alternative to the more common pattern of separate worship and Sunday school.

6. A youth coffee house has been established in the West Mall by the Anglican Church, but is financially failing and staffed inadequately. It is only able to open its doors on Thursday and Saturday evenings. The City Youth Service has offered to train counsellors in a course over several months.

7. The Church of Christ near Central has a small modern "round" church, suitable for innovative worship with families.

8. The Roman Catholic school near North has a large, well equipped auditorium with a well equipped stage, and would let us use it.

9. The Children's Theatre has approached Central for the use of facilities for a vacation crafts and recreation school for children of the area. (They use paid tutors and fees are charged to cover costs.) Their ventures elsewhere have been very successful.

10. The neighbouring parish (in an expanding suburb to the west) has a strong youth work program involving young people from age 13, using small cell groups. It is attracting many of the youth of our church families.

11. A Lutheran Church (near East) with a failing congregation, has a suitable church building, hall and adequate grounds to consider the possibility of developing an all-day-care centre for children. (East would need expensive modifications before it could be used for such a purpose.)

12. The local Baptist Church has a small congregation near Central with a Sunday school which is very small. They are served by the Baptist minister from the City Baptist Church. They have been asking your minister if there are ways to co-operate.

13.

14.

TASK FORCE TWO

1. Each church in the parish has its own Council of Elders and Property Committee, as well as Stewardship, Mission, Social Responsibility, Christian education, Flower, Music and Fair committees. All of these meet regularly.

2. Outside groups use our facilities:
    Central is used by a weekly A.A. meeting, and by a ballet dancing class two afternoons a week.
    North is used by an aerobics class three mornings a week.
    The Jungian Society meets fortnightly in the evening at East.

3. The Council of Elders at Central has talked about taking greater pastoral responsibility for members of the congregation.

4. A married couple at Central have told their elder about the small "support group" to which they belonged in their former church. The group met fortnightly and met a need which is not being fulfilled in this parish.

5. Some members who participated in the ecumenical discussion groups in preparation for the World Council of Churches Assembly in Canberra are asking when we might do something like this again.

6. Financial giving has remained at the same level as last year, though the expenditure of the parish has increased by more than 10%. Our wider giving will have to be drastically cut to maintain the present local expenditure.

7. The church at Central needs major repairs at a considerable expense, which will require a loan. The large Sunday school hall and rooms are in good condition. The building at East also needs repairs. The buildings at North are in excellent condition, but still carry a considerable debt.

8. Each church in the parish has an evening Fellowship Group, meeting monthly. These are supposed to be for both women and men, but North is the only one that actually has men among its membership. All groups are complaining about poor attendances.

9. Child baptisms, confirmations, weddings and funerals are a regular part of parish life.

10. There are three identical worship services in the parish each Sunday.

11. The small but active parish youth fellowship meets weekly at Central.

12. Over recent years a number of key people have moved away from the parish. New people coming in have not offset the losses.

13.

14.

TASK FORCE THREE

1. Some families are travelling in to Central from their new homes in the expanding suburbs to the west of the parish. Increasingly, however, these families are becoming irregular in attendance at worship.

2. On the city side of Central there are many new flats being constructed, but few members are residing there.

3. Several members of East are very involved in the Meals on Wheels project which operates from the Salvation Army centre nearby.

4. The eastern area of the parish has old housing, and a rapidly changing population, the latest of whom are of Indo-chinese origin. Houses are being coverted to flats. Complaints are reported in the newspaper of high rents and poor conditions.

5. The membership at East has declined to a few older life-long residents. Parish Council has suggested that worship services there be terminated, but the East Elders are against this.

6. There is a grant available for development of a child-care centre for pre-school children in an area close to industry. It will require a 20% matching of funds or resources by the organisation which receives the grant.

7. There are evening community course available on human relationships and on social problems.

8. The Eastern area, having an increased migrant population, needs a special ministry. Our parish does not have the resources, but the Presbytery may be able to raise the resources for a community lay worker.

9. A member of Central has a large, unused, one-room repair shop next to his house a couple of blocks away from the church.

10. Mr Fitzroy, a member of North, is a lecturer in children's education at the Teachers College. He has offered his services one evening a week.

11. Dr Gwen Goldwin, a practising psychiatrist and a member of North, has offered to share her consultative skills on one evening a week, if a referral system could be organised.

12. Sunday morning sport for boys and girls is increasing, and the Sunday school teachers are complaining about irregular attendance by most children.

13.

14.

The discipleship game

A game about being Christian by Pat Baker

Number of players: up to 15.

You will need: a large copy of the game board, a counter for each player, a single die. You may like to colour the shaded squares on the game board.

Aim

The aim of the game is to win by collecting a full set of seven different DISCIPLESHIP cards. Along the way participants will do some thinking and talking about what discipleship means for them in various areas of their life.

Process and rules

1. Set up the board, with the stack of DISCIPLESHIP cards face down nearby.

2. Decide who will start. Each player places a counter on any one of the coloured (shaded) squares (only one counter to a square). If there are more than ten players the later ones must wait until others have moved off the starting squares.

3. The first player throw the die and moves the number of squares indicated. The move may be in any direction, but only connecting

squares may be used and players may not reverse direction in the middle of a move (though they may go the opposite way next time). Each player throws and moves.

4. When someone lands on a square marked with a cross they take the top DISCIPLESHIP card from the pack. They read it aloud and tell the group what discipleship means for them in that area of their life. They keep the card.

5. Anyone landing on a square marked OOPS! must return one DISCIPLESHIP card to the bottom of the pack.

6. A player landing on a square marked CHANGE must change one of his or her DISCIPLESHIP cards, either by arranging a trade with another player or by returning the card to the bottom of the pack and replacing it with the top card. In the case of a trade, both players must say what discipleship means for them in the area for which they are receiving a card. If the player chooses to take a card from the pack, he or she must tell the group in the usual way what discipleship means for them in that area of their life.

7. When a player receives a card which is a duplicate of one they already have, they must not simply repeat what they said before, but must find something new to say about their discipleship in that area.

8. Players may not land on or pass through a square occupied by another player's counter. If a player is blocked so that it is impossible for them to complete a move they must go to the nearest coloured (shaded) square and pay the penalty (see rule 9).

9. After the beginning of the game anyone landing on a coloured (shaded) square must return **all** his or her DISCIPLESHIP cards to the bottom of the pack.

10. The winner is the first player to collect a complete set of seven DISCIPLESHIP cards.

11. In order to keep the game flowing it is a good idea to limit players to ten seconds per move after throwing the die. This may be timed by the leader, or the other players may count aloud. Anyone not completing a move within the time limit must return one DISCIPLESHIP card to the bottom of the pack.

The discipleship cards

Prepare a set of 70 cards, each approximately 7cm x 4cm. There will be ten cards for each of the following seven areas of life:
LIFE STYLE
RELATIONSHIPS
STEWARDSHIP
WITNESS
CHURCH INVOLVEMENT
SPIRITUAL LIFE
VOCATION

If there are other areas which may be especially important for members of your group, feel free to substitute them for some of the areas listed here.

After the game

Some of the things that happened during the course of the game may call for discussion. For example:

- What experiences in real life may be compared with losing one or more of your discipleship cards?

- Did you feel that you were competing against the other players? Does this really happen in your Christian life?

- Did your advance ever lead to someone else's downfall? Did you foresee this? If so, why did you choose the course you took? Would you act like this in real life?

- Did you ever forego an advantage for the sake of another player? If so, why?

- What aspects of your discipleship did you find it easiest to talk about? Which were hardest?

First published in YOUTHLEADER Issue 27, May 1983 (JBCE).

the discipleship game

by Pat Baker

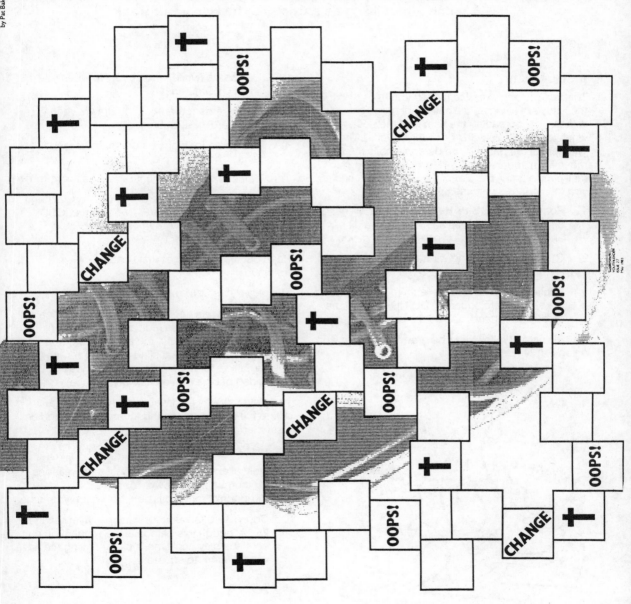

Spread the flame!

A game about living as a Christian by Harry Burgraaf

Instructions

This is a gaming exercise to help you think through the issues of living as a Christian and being a witness, or "spreading the flame" of the gospel, in what you do and say in your everyday life. The "winner" of the game is the person who is the first to move from square 1 to 25. However, winning isn't really important – the aim of the game is to enable you to share and discuss.

1. Form groups of 5 to 10. Each group will need a playing board, three sets of cards, a dice, and a counter for each person in the group.

2. Choose a leader who will keep time and direct the action of the game.

3. Shuffle the cards and place them face down on the appropriate squares. DO NOT look at the cards beforehand. Cards are of three types:

SHARE cards (yellow) – to be drawn when you land on an EVEN number

INVOLVE cards (white) – to be drawn when you land on an ODD number

SURPRISE cards (green) – to be drawn when you land on a SURPRISE square.

4. Throw dice for highest number to see who starts. Then each player in turn:

Throw dice to determine number of spaces to move.

Pick up the appropriate card (SHARE – yellow on an EVEN number; INVOLVE – white on an ODD number; SURPRISE – green on a SURPRISE square).

Read out the question or instruction (unless told not to) aloud.

The player has ONE minute to think and answer.

If a white card has been picked up the leader calls VOTE and other players indicate thumbs UP (if they are satisfied or agree with the answer), thumbs DOWN (if they are dissatisfied or disagree with the answer), arms folded (if they are undecided – undecided people move back ONE space).

The player moves backward or forward by the difference of thumbs up and thumbs down, and as instructed by cards.

Return used card to the bottom of the pile.

5. Only after voting do you discuss the reasons for thumbs up or down. Use this as an opportunity for discussion, but watch your time.

6. Continue to move in turn until a player reaches 25. Although this person is the winner you can continue play until time is up by having the winner return to square 1.

1	2	surprise	4	5
6	7	surprise	9	10
surprise	12	13	14	15
surprise	17	18	surprise	20
21	22	23	surprise	25

involve ~ odd	share ~ even	surprise
white	yellow	green

P

SHARE Cards

After the Apostle Peter denied that he knew Jesus or cared about him, he regretted it deeply.
Can you think of a time or occasion when you "denied" Jesus, either in actual words or by your actions?

A commitment to Christ is a commitment to being a servant. How easy or hard, natural or unnatural, do you find it to "serve" another person or other people, in the spirit of Jesus who washed his disciples' feet.
Why, how come?

What is your attitude to the church and the church's task of mission to the world at this point in time?

Share the details of an outreach service or mission event you have been involved in in some way.
If you haven't been involved at all, indicate why you would or wouldn't like to do something which "spreads the flame" of the gospel.

Share some things you like or appreciate about your family.

The book of Acts talks about old people dreaming dreams and young people having visions.
What "visions" and "dreams" for a better world or society do you have, if any? Don't just think of grand changes. What specific things in the world would you like to see changed?

What we need is Christian nurses, artists, plumbers, football players, computer programmers and so on who, in the ordinary course of their lives and activities, demonstrate what it means to belong to God and the Kingdom.
What is one area of your life where you can make a Christian contribution?

What does it mean to you personally when the Bible says that "you are the light of the world" and "you are the salt of the earth"?

Can you think of one area of life, an event you've participated in, a decision you've made, in which belonging to God and being a Christian made a difference in what you did or decided?
Share the details.

What sort of things help you or hinder you in being a witness for Jesus in your daily life?

Share an experience, incident or occasion where you have had to defend, stand up for or explain your relationship with God or involvement in church.

Share some of the hassles or difficulties you have about being a Christian – or your joys and excitement if they are more frequent.

How do you feel about talking about God and sharing your faith with your friends, particularly your non-Christian friends?

What is one thing that you have discovered from the Bible recently?

How concerned are you about some of the injustices in our society (poor people, people who can't afford accomodation, Aborignal heal, exploited young people etc)?
Share what you've thought and done in this area if anything.

What are the three most iportant things in your life right now?

How much do world problems such as famine, war, refugees, violence etc figure in your thoughts and prayers?

What things about your life at the moment will indicate to people at work or school that you are a Christian – or not interested in Christian things?

Can you think of any ways in which you have made life more pleasant, enjoyable or attractive for another person recently?

The Bible talks about "righteous anger".
Is there anything recently that has made you rightly angry (in the news, at work, in society)? Would God have been angry about it too?

You have a good friend who is not a Christian. You often see each other and do a lot of things together. How can you share your love for Jesus and your Christian faith (if you are a Christian) in a way which is sensitive and respects your friend's views and feelings?

If you are a member of a youth group you get a lot of benefit out of being together – learning and growing, belonging, friendship, struggling through spiritual issues together. What sort of practical things can a Christian youth group do to "spread the flame" of the gospel to people your own age in your local community?

In your trade or profession or place of employment it is compulsory to be a member of a trade union. How do you respond to this as a Christian? If you decide to join, how can you make a positive contribution?

How can Christians show that they live by God's values and principles in the way they use their time? Give practical examples.

You are a member of a cricket, footy, netball (or whatever you're in to) team. The game used to be a lot of fun, but it's getting more and more competitive and cut-throat. So much so that winning is more important than the game itself. There's a lot of cheating, abuse of umpires, and excessively rough behaviour. How does a Christian handle that? How can he/she be a witness in sport?

In your city or town most young people wouldn't be seen dead in a church and care little about God. If you are a Christian what sort of responsibilities do you have for people of your own age in your community who don't know God?

You have just turned 18 and are allowed to vote in the next election. How does being a Christian make any difference in the issues you consider and in how and who you vote for?

Name an important social problem in your local community (town, city, district). What should the church and/or your youth group be doing about it? What could they be doing about it?

You are finding things a little difficult at home. Communication between you and your parents isn't what it could be. You feel your parents have unreal expectations about hours of coming home, letting them know where you're going, your friends and activities. What might you do? What's a Christian response?

Buying a car is buying a car no matter who does it. Or does a Christian consider different factors than someone who has no commitment to God and Christian values when it comes to cars? Can a Christian be a witness in her/his attitude to buying and using a car? What do you think?

A community survey shows that there are many lonely, elderly people in your district who find it difficult to get out and about. What might a Christian response involve?

There are thousands of young people today who are homeless for various reasons. Should Christians be concerned about this? What practical things can we do about it?

Your mates at school or work often talk about war, nuclear arms and the immense amounts of money spent on weapons. One day some of them invite you to participate in a "peace march" in the city on a Saturday afternoon. What do you decide and why?

You have just finished your final year at school. Friends talk about finding a job which will pay well, provides good conditions, short hours and lots of satisfaction. What factors does a Christian consider in choosing a job or vocation?

Your friends at work or school throw a New Years Eve party and you are invited. Can you be a witness there in a positive way? How?

Christians are a witness in the world – not just through words about the gospel, but by doing everything they do with gusto, creativity, style and according to God's pattern for things. What is one area of life where you think Christians could be a better witness in this sense, and how?

48

Your town or city has a large group of unemployed youth. They are bored, vandalise property, hang around the pinball parlours with nothing to do, and generally "waste" their lives. What can your church or youth group do to help these young people? Do we have a responsibility to help?

How can a Christian muso or artist or architect or builder show through their art or work that this world belongs to God and that God is redeeming it?

From your local newspaper you learn that there are a growing number of homeless young people in your district. What sort of responsibility, if any, does your youth group and church have to these young people? What can you do?

Someone in your youth group has been reading up about rock music and becomes convinced that with back-masking, the occult, suggestive lyrics and so on, rock music is evil. He suggests at a youth group discussion that you all should get rid of your rock records and tapes. What do you say? What is a Christian response to rock?

Several members of your youth group are going steady. Although it is never openly discussed, it is an accepted fact that some of the couples regularly sleep together. You've had a series of topics at youth group on sexuality and relationships, and everyone says "the right thing" in discussion. You wonder about the hypocrisy of it all. What is your response?

One evening you see a powerful documentary on poverty and famine in Africa. At the end of the program there is a plea for financial and practical help. You've just saved up enough money to buy an expensive new stereo system. How do you respond?

You've been knocking around with a group of people who aren't Christians. One day the subject of religion comes up in conversation. Someone says, "I don't see how anyone today could possibly believe in God". How do you respond?

You have been having a series of topics on "Mission" at your youth group. One evening a visiting speaker shares the need for Christian teachers, carpenters, printers, doctors, pastors and others in overseas countries and issues a challening call for youth group members to consider overseas service. How do you respond? What factors do you consider?

At work (school) a group of you are discussing movies and videos. Some people describe the "R" and "X" rated material they've been watching. How do you participate in the discussion? What is a Christian response to films?

A group of you have been to see a film about apartheid in South Africa. One person in the group says, "I think apartheid is OK – blacks need to be kept in their place". Another person in the group angrily responds that apartheid is evil and we should do everything in our power to see it abolished. What's your response?

P

Your church is situated in an area where there are lots of children and younger teenagers. There seems to be little for them to do. As a youth group you've been thinking about your responsibility to the community. What can you do?

A group of your "mates" from church spend Saturday evening at the local pub and disco. You know some of them get quite drunk and one has been convicted of drink driving. They've invited you to join them several times and ask you again to come next Saturday. What's your response?

You find the church deadly dull. Worship seems to be uninspiring and the activities don't seem to meet your needs. You just feel uninvolved and unmotivated. How might you go about changing the situation?

One of the local charismatic churches is organising a "Torch run for Jesus". It'll be a march through the city with banners and singing, ending in a community concert. You're invited to participate – individually and as a group. How do you respond to such a public Christian witness?

You're on a long bus journey on your way home from a holiday. You're sitting next to someone approximately your own age. Do you use this as an opportunity for evangelism – why or why not? How?

You attend a meeting of the congregation of your church. During the business the matter of financial support for youth activities is discussed. One of the older people stands up and says that youth don't need or deserve financial support – they're apathetic, do nothing for the church in any case, and are irresponsible. How do you respond?

Your church has been invited to make a creative contribution to a community festival being organised by the local council. It is to be a multicultural event in an outside venue. What might you do to make an input for the gospel?

You attend an interdenominational rally where the speaker addresses the theme "Live simple, so that others may simply live". What might the practical implications of that be in your life and the life of your youth group?

There are a number of young people who have begun attending church more or less regularly but are not involved in any other church activities and – as far as you can see – don't seem to feel the need for active commitment to the church or to Jesus Christ. How might you convince them?

SURPRISE cards

Think of a biblical story, parable or proverb. Mime it for the other members of the group.
If another group member can guess what the parable or story is you can move forward two squares and the first person to guess it can move forward one square.

You are all too engrossed in the game; you need a breather. Go for a run around the building, all holding hands.
All move forward one space.

Sad surprise. All members of the group move back by half the squares you have come so far (i.e. if you're on square 8 you move back to 4; if you're on square 11 you move back to 5 etc.).

Imagine that your group has been asked to nominate a young person from your group to attend a world conference on "How youth can serve their local communities".
Think for a while about qualifications needed. Then each person in the group indicate who they nominate and why. The person with the most nominations moves forward two spaces.

DO NOT READ THIS ALOUD
You have one minute to get everyone in the group laughing.
If you succeed, move forward two spaces. If you fail, move back one space for each person not laughing. Play can continue while you try, or you can stop the proceedings to get the laughs.

Something sad has occurred. The other members of your group have been struck blind and you are the only one left who can see.
Make everyone close their eyes. Then, by verbal instructions, lead all the others to the group sitting furthest away from you. Introduce them to one of those people by describing the person. Then go back to the game.
Group members must keep their eyes closed for the whole time.

Have a break. Play leapfrog.
Leapfrog over each other, all taking part, for about 100 metres and then back again. Say "Hi" to any other groups you meet on the way.

DO NOT READ THIS ALOUD
Think of a pleasant surprise you can give someone else in the group right now. Give the surprise. Then ask other members of the group to vote on whether it was a pleasant surprise or not. Move forward or backward by the balance of yes and no votes.

Use your imagination. Within two minutes give each person in your group a nickname. Then get them to indicate if they think the nickname is appropriate or not. Move forward or back by the balance of yes and no answers.

Go to another group and introduce yourselves. Decide on an acitivity which will take no longer than one minute and do it all together (i.e. both groups). All move forward one space (both groups).

The Christian life is about servanthood, which can sometimes be sacrificial and demanding.
All swap places on the board with the person sitting on your left. Start with the youngest member of the group and go around the group in a clockwise direction.

Stand in a circle and hold hands. Sing and dance "Ring around a rosie" and, after falling down, all move back 5 spaces.

Sorry, no surprise this time. However, you and one other person you choose can move forward one space.

As a group form the tallest tower you can, using every member of the group. While you are in position, sing a song.
All move forward one space.

Lead the group in an activity of your choosing which takes no more than two minutes. If the majority of the group like it after they've done it (vote yes/no) you can move forward two spaces. If the majority don't like it, move back two spaces.

All stand and yell at the top of your voices: "We love this game! We love this game!" If any of the other groups turn around to see what's going on, all move forward one space; if they indicate no interest, all move back one space.

Cave-in

A game about survival and values by Pat Baker

The game

1. Sit close together in one corner of the room, on the floor if possible. Turn out the lights, pull down the blinds, or otherwise make the room as dark as possible. Put a lighted candle in the centre of the group. Read the situation aloud.

2. Go around the circle, one at a time, giving reasons why you should be at the head of the line. Your reasons can be of two kinds. You can say what you want to live for: or what you have yet to get out of life that is important to you. Or you can talk about what you have to contribute to others in the world that would justify your being near the front of the line. Both types of reasons will be considered equally; the things you want to live for can have just as much weight as the things you could do for others. You may choose to pass; although in this situation a pass means you are deciding to allow yourself to be placed near the end of the line.

3. Decide on the order of the line. Try to reach agreement by some way other than voting.

The situation

The group, on an outing to some caves, has been trapped hundreds of feet below ground by a cave-in. There is a narrow passageway leading up and out of the cavern where you are trapped. Night is coming fast and there is no one around for miles to help. You decide to form a single file and try to work your way out of the cave. But at any moment there might be another rock slide. The ones nearest to the front of the line will have the best chances for survival. Each group member will give his or her reasons for wanting to be at the head of the line. After hearing each other's reasons, you will determine the order by which you will file out.

Evaluation

When the order has been decided (or when you have reached a point where you simply cannot decide), put on the lights, put out the candle, and discuss the game:

- How did you feel about the game?
- Were the reasons you gave for being allowed a chance to live the real reasons? If not, why not?
- What difficulties did you have in deciding the order?
- What did the game teach you about yourself?

First published in SURVIVAL PLUS in the Youth Elective Series (JBCE).

Projects for a new world

A game about working for a better world

Purpose

To provide an opportunity for participants to consider some general trends in the modern world as a whole, and some ways in which individuals or groups can try to affect the course of events. The game also provides an opportunity for participants to reflect more closely on their own personal priorities and concerns.

Preparation

Four outlines of real or imaginary "projects for change" are needed. Some imaginary projects are described in the group role profiles below. These descriptions can be used as they stand, or adapted, or imitated. Aid agencies and social welfare organisations will be able to provide information about real projects which could be substituted for the imaginary ones.

You will also need to designate meeting areas for the groups involved in the game. Each area should be identified by a large label. A table in the central meeting area should be labelled "Grants Committee". Other labels should relate to the particular project being advocated by the group meeting in that place.

Scenario

Your organisation has money to give away! You want to do it responsibly, putting the money where it will do the most good in making the world a better place. Consequently you have set up a Grants Committee to examine all applications and suggestions for distribution of the money and to make the final decision. Various lobby groups within the organisation are promoting different projects as worthy recipients of aid.

Participants will be assigned roles as members of the Grants Committee or one of the lobby groups. After working out strategies in their own group, they

will take part in a public meeting where each lobby group will present its proposal and the Grants Committee will hand down its decision.

Procedure

1. Introduce the game by outlining the scenario above.

2. Divide the participants into five groups, not necessarily of equal numbers. The Grants Committee should have no more than six members. Lobby groups may have any number.

3. Give an envelope containing a group role profile to each group. The lobby groups will also receive a copy of the grant application which they will be asked to support. The Grants Committee will receive copies of all four grant applications. Say that the envelopes are not to be opened until groups have moved to their designated meeting places.

4. Say that groups have 15 minutes in which to read their group role profile and prepare their strategy for the public meeting. At the end of that time there will be a signal to call them back to the central meeting place.

5. After 15 minutes, give the signal for re-assembly. Allow 2 or 3 minutes for participants to settle. Then hand over to the Grants Committee to conduct the public meeting. (Each lobby group should be given an opportunity to present its proposal to the Grants Committee. The Grants Commitee may cross-examine any or all of the lobby groups.)

6. The Grants Committee deliberates (in public) and announces its decision.

Discussion

Follow-up discussion is likely to concentrate mainly on the reasons which participants give for their decisions. What factors do they take into account? And what relative weight do they give to these factors? With regard to the four imaginary projects outlined in the group role profiles, for example, what is their view (if any) of factors such as the following?

- status and respectability of the people arranging the project
- the number of people likely to be deeply affected
- the number of people likely to be slightly affected
- the actual subject-matter of the project
- the political views expressed or implied in the proposals
- the timescale involved
- the problems of evaluating the success of the project
- the problems of communicating information about the project to others
- the possible harm which the project might do
- the extent, if any, to which they personally would like to take an active part in the project
- the extent, if any, to which they might personally be affected by the project.

Group profile: GRANTS COMMITTEE

Your organisation has $10,000 to distribute to worthwhile projects. You have been appointed to examine all grant applications and to decide on allocations. Lobby groups within the organisation support each of the four applications that have been received. You have called a public meeting at which the lobby groups will present their proposals and you will have the opportunity to cross-examine them before making your decision.

You have the power to allocate the $10,000 as you see fit once you have heard from the lobby groups.

In preparation for the public meeting you should decide on procedure, e.g. choose someone to chair the meeting, decide whether cross-examination will be conducted by one appointed person or by anyone who has a question.

You will also need to read all the grant applications and draw up a list of questions to be put to their supporters.

Group role profile: WORK

You know that your organisation has $10,000 to distribute to projects approved by the Grants Committee. You are concerned about youth unemployment and believe that a substantial grant should be given to the young people who submitted the enclosed application to your organisation. Other groups will be advocating different proposals, so you will need a strong argument to convince the Grants Committee to support the work project. Use the time before the public meeting
a) to make a list of points to back up this application
b) to decide how you will put them to the committee.

Group role profile: FESTIVAL CENTRES

You know that your organisation has $10,000 to distribute to projects approved by the Grants Committee. You are concerned about the future of the Planet Earth and believe that a substantial grant should be given to the man who submitted the enclosed application to your organisation. Other groups will be advocating different proposals, so you will need a strong argument to convince the Grants Committee to support the festival centres project. Use the time before the public meeting
a) to make a list of points to back up this application
b) to decide how you will put them to the committee.

Group role profile: SCHOOL

You know that your organisation has $10,000 to distribute to projects approved by the Grants Committee. You are concerned about the dehumanising effects of bigness and believe that a substantial grant should be given to the person who submitted the enclosed application to your organisation. Other groups will be advocating different proposals, so you will need a strong argument to convince the Grants Committee to support the school project. Use the time before the public meeting
a) to make a list of points to back up this application
b) to decide how you will put them to the committee.

Group role profile: MUSIC & THEATRE

You know that your organisation has $10,000 to distribute to projects approved by the Grants Committee. You are concerned about the Third World and believe that a substantial grant should be given to the people who submitted the enclosed application to your organisation, as they obviously have a message to present. Other groups will be advocating different proposals, so you will need a strong argument to convince the Grants Committee to support the music and theatre project. Use the time before the public meeting
a) to make a list of points to back up this application
b) to decide how you will put them to the committee.

Grant application: WORK

There are very few jobs going in this place. Especially young people can't get jobs. We're some of them. There are 8 of us. Ages 16-18. We can't get work. The situation is even worse now that one of the biggest factories round here is due to close. The head office of the firm is hundreds of kilometres away. They couldn't care less about us. They're just interested in what makes money for them.

No one is going to help us. We've just got to help ourselves. We want to get our own business together. It won't be anything special. But something's better than nothing. Running a cafe. Decorating, cleaning the town up, some building jobs. Collecting and sorting "rubbish" and selling it. Growing food on "waste" land around here. There are lots of things we can do. But definitely we need some money to get us started.

Grant application: FESTIVAL CENTRES

I'm a businessman. I have a lot of experience of fund-raising. I want to launch a really big appeal for money. About one hundred million dollars, from people all over the world. And then with this money I want to set up some *Planet Earth Festival Centres*. Each centre will be a fabulous mixture of funfair, zoo, park, museum, education centre, holiday camp. A place where people come to really enjoy themselves. But where they also learn about what's going on on Planet Earth. The problems of the world. And the background to them. And how they can be solved. And how everyone's got a part to play. And there's no need to get miserable and depressed.

But first, I need some money to get an Appeal Committee together and to start work.

Grant application: SCHOOL

I write as the principal of a secondary school, and on behalf of the whole staff.

In our view the worst problem in the modern world is that everything has grown so big. Big blocks of flats, big motorways, big schools, big factories, big companies, big organisations, big cities. Everything's getting so faceless and impersonal. Nobody cares about anybody else. Nobody is able really to be their own boss, live their own life.

The answer is to re-create villages. "Small is beautiful." Human beings need to live in much smaller communities. Back to the countryside – but also we need to break cities up into small communities. Then each community will organise itself in its own way, and have power over its own affairs.

At this school we want to make a start on this task of creating small communities, and giving people more control over their own lives. We should like to grow a lot of our own food here, for a start. We should also like to experiment with non-violent technology – wind pump, a water turbine, a methane generator, a solar collector etc. So that at least students know how they work. And we should like to accept responsibility for disposing of our own waste.

Slowly and surely we should like to change our school into a much more self-reliant community than it is at present. We want to be pioneers, trying to create a new sort of society. And trying, all the time, to learn. But we need some money to get started ...

Grant application: MUSIC & THEATRE

There are six of us – three men, three girls. We're a pop group, we also act and dance. We've written this musical play about world trade. About how difficult it is for poorer countries to get decent prices for tea, coffee, sugar, copper, sisal, jute, cotton etc. And about how difficult it is for them to make and sell their own manufactured goods. And also about how the richer people in these countries often don't do anything to help the poorer ones.

Our play tries to wake people up to what's going on in the world. So that people won't be sheep, just accepting things as they are. We want to put on our play all over the country. In pubs, schools, canteens, shopping centres, everywhere people meet. We don't want to charge admission, so we need some money to cover our transport and food for an 8-week tour in the summer.

Adapted from LEARNING FOR CHANGE IN WORLD SOCIETY (London: World Studies Project, 1976.)

The family game

A game by Brian W. M. and Janet Smith, designed for use at a family camp

Rules of the games

1. About six players are needed.

2. Decide length of time for the game – e.g. one hour.

3. Using pencils and pad each player may jot down comments or questions to be shared/asked when his or her turn comes.

4. Each player places a playing piece at "START".

5. Place two sets of cards on the board:

   – "What do you think?" cards

   – "That's life" cards.

6. Anyone can begin by throwing the dice and moving the playing piece according to the number turned up. The player to the left has the next turn.

7. When you land on a "What do you think?" space, draw a card from the pile of that name. Turn it over and read it aloud. Answer honestly, giving an explanation if you wish.

8. When you land on a "Your choice" space you have several choices:

   – You may make any comment you wish on any subject.

   – You may ask someone a question that he or she may answer briefly without waiting for their turn.

   – You may draw a "What do you think?" card and follow the instructions in 7 above.

9. When you land on a "That's life" space, pick up a "That's life" card, turn it over, read it aloud and respond accordingly. On your next turn, follow the arrow out of the place on the board to which you have been sent.

10. Listen to one another and try to accept and understand the feelings shared by others.

11. Winning is not important. Contributing is important.

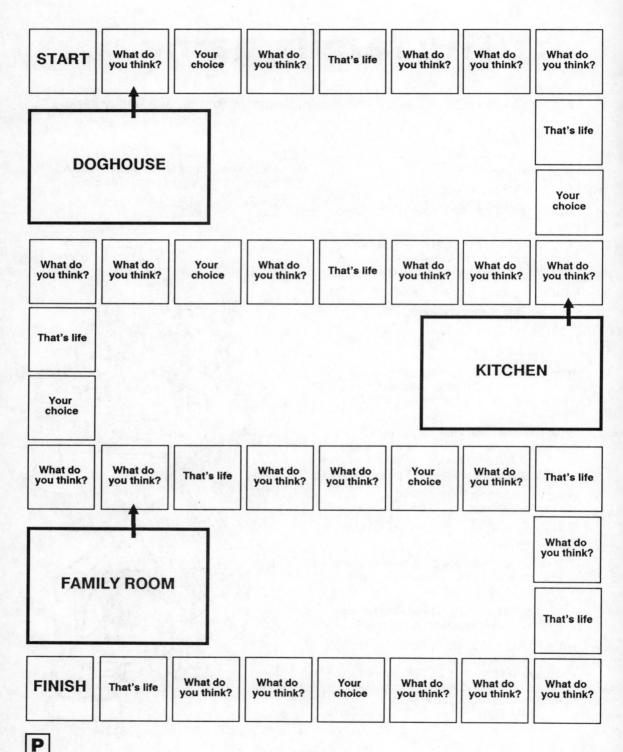

START | What do you think? | Your choice | What do you think? | That's life | What do you think? | What do you think? | What do you think?

DOGHOUSE

That's life

Your choice

What do you think? | What do you think? | Your choice | What do you think? | That's life | What do you think? | What do you think? | What do you think?

That's life

Your choice

KITCHEN

What do you think? | What do you think? | That's life | What do you think? | What do you think? | Your choice | What do you think? | That's life

What do you think?

That's life

FAMILY ROOM

FINISH | That's life | What do you think? | What do you think? | Your choice | What do you think? | What do you think? | What do you think?

P

THAT'S LIFE CARDS

If you tried to make someone happy today, go to the FAMILY ROOM.

If you have cheered someone up this week, go to the FAMILY ROOM.

If you have left your bed unmade or your room (etc.) untidy today, go into the DOGHOUSE.

If you have told someone a funny story this weekend (or today), go to the FAMILY ROOM.

If you have introduced yourself to someone new this weekend (or today), go to the KITCHEN.

If you have not had a talk with someone under 10 **and** someone over 50 this weekend (or today), go to the KITCHEN.

If you have noticed something beautiful today, go to the FAMILY ROOM.

If you felt lonely this week, go and enjoy the company in THE FAMILY ROOM. Take with you the player whose token is closest to yours.

If you have missed your turn to do the dishes (or feed the dog etc.) this week, go into DOGHOUSE.

If you have not complimented someone today, go to the KITCHEN.

If you always put the top back on the toothpaste tube, have an extra turn.

If you have not laughed aloud today, go to the KITCHEN.

If you haven't yet done a favour for someone today, go to the KITCHEN.

If you have felt fearful this week, you might benefit by company! Ask the player whose token is on or nearest to the KITCHEN to go with you to the FAMILY ROOM.

If you have complained today, go into the DOGHOUSE.

Introduce yourself and tell the group **one** thing your family likes about you.

WHAT DO YOU THINK? CARDS

NOTE: These cards were designed with youth and adult participants in mind. If the game is to be used with children you will need to alter wording on many of them.

How can Christian parents pass on their faith to their children?

What things are most important for the happiness of the family?

What priority do family commitments take in your life?

Should Christian families have times for sharing their faith and Christian experiences?

What is the role of the family in our culture/society?

Do you see any threat(s) to the survival of the family?

Is everyone of equal importance in the family?

How important are grandparents?

What is your definition of a good child?

What is your definition of a good mother?

Should all members of a family have designated responsibilities or jobs?

What can we do as Christians to reach out to people who have no natural family?

Does the church help to build up strong family life? How?

What is your definition of a good father?

Who is the head of the family?

What/who is a family?

Why is secure family life important to children?

What bit of advice would you give to a young man about to get married?

What do you think about when you can't fall asleep?

Talk about a happy marriage.

Share a time when you had hurt feelings.

What advice would you give to a young woman about to get married?

What does this mean to you: "Bear one another's burdens" (Galatians 6:2)?

Describe the perfect wife.

What is the best thing about love?

How would you define love?

What do you think is your purpose in life?

What is your most sentimental possession?

When do you feel frustrated?

What four things are most important in your life?

Share an experience of answered prayer.

Describe your life at age 70.

What fruit of the Spirit do you most need right now in your life. (Love, joy, peace, patience, kindness, generosity, faithfulness, tolerance, self-control – Galatians 5:22.)

When do you feel sad?

What do you dislike most about yourself?

Of all your material possessions, what do you enjoy the most?

What life dream are you still trying to make come true?

Describe a happy family.

Complete the statement: "If I could live my life over again ... "

How do you feel when someone laughs at you?

_____

What is the worst thing parents can do to children?

_____

Give three words to describe how you feel right now.

_____

Complete the statement: "One thing I missed during my childhood was ... "

_____

When do you get angry?

_____

Describe the perfect husband.

_____

What seems to complicate your life?

_____

If you could hang a motto or saying in every home in the world, what would it be?

_____

How do you feel about growing old?

_____

What is needed in homes and families to make them really happy and comfortable for those in them?

_____

How can Christians share their family life with others?

_____

Complete the following: "My prayer for my family is ... "

_____

Complete the following: "The ideal family ... "

_____

At what stage do dependent children become independent adults?

_____

Complete the following: "The trouble with some families ... "

_____

How can the Christian faith be significant in family life?

_____

Describe your role as a member of a family.

_____

Who should make decisions about what children do?

_____

Tell of an exciting or humorous incident which occurred in your family.

_____

What things can you suggest as helpful in building family life?

_____

Make policy, not coffee

A game designed to air the variety of opinions on how women can achieve equal status in society by Kathy Brophy Frick

Number

Any number can play. If you have more than five players, divide up into teams. We played with four teams of five people each – which provided lots of opinions and talk. Our players were faculty and staff from the university and public school teachers from the area. All were interested in non-sexist education.

Begin

To begin, each player makes a list of five policies that they think would bring women into equal status in society. If you're playing in teams, each team makes one list. The policy can be at any level of generality and realism – "Legislate for equal rights", for example, or "Raise all children to be non-sexist".

Each policymaker assumes unlimited personal power – they assume they can implement whatever they can imagine. When each person has finished their list of five policies, the group draws up a common list. Each person contributes one item from their list.

That policy is written in abbreviated form on a chalkboard or chart. In the game we played, one team offered this policy: "Institute a system of alimony based on the person's need for money until he/she can be educated for work". This was listed as "Limited alimony". Continue listing, going around the group as many times as necessary, until you have ten policies.

Continue

Now you're ready for the exciting part. Set aside your own list and study the common one. Try to figure out which item will be the most acceptable to people playing the game. Which policy will appeal to the most people? Each person or team picks one. Write down the number of the policy, but keep it covered until everybody has decided. Then show your numbers to one another.

Your score for the round is based on how many people picked the same number you did. In our first round, three groups picked "Pass the Equal Rights Amendment" as the most popular policy and one group picked "Adequate day care". The ERA groups scored three points apiece and the day care group scored one point.

After you record your score, write the most popular policy in a new list and cross it off the common list. "Pass the Equal Rights Amendment" thus went at the head of our new list.

Now try to figure out the second most popular policy from the nine choices you have left. In our second round, the vote was a tie: two votes for "Adequate day care" and two votes for "End institutionalised sex-stereotyping". So we had a 3-minute discussion during which each team argued for its policy.

The "adequate day care" group asserted: "Many women could find satisfying work outside the home if they knew their children would be getting good care". But the "end stereotyping" proponents argued: "Day care only affects families with young children. If we abolished sex stereotyping it would change many people's lives."

The recount showed that the stereotyping groups swayed the voting 4-0 – and four points for each team.

Now you go on to the third round. The game is played for five rounds.

Policymakers and problem solvers

To find out who won, add up your scores from the five rounds. The highest score wins. This person or team is the one with the best feel for public opinion on the issue. It is the one who can spot the popular policies on the list. We'll call this person a "policymaker".

There is another winner too. Look at your original list. How many of your own original policies are listed in the top five? That number is your "problem solvers" score.

The highest score belongs to the person who can generate the most appealing ways to solve problems. You'll probably find that the "policymakers" and the "problem solvers" are different people; each seems to be a distinct talent.

More policies, more coffee

For your second and third go-rounds, try these variations:

1. Take the top policy from the previous game. Make the object of the game the development of more detailed ways to accomplish that aim. After one session of MAKE POLICY, NOT COFFEE, the top policy was "Guarantee equal opportunity in every aspect of life". In our second round, we came up with detailed ways to accomplish equality of opportunity: "Free day care for working parents" was popular, and so was "quality education for every person".

2. After each vote for the more detailed way to proceed, have a 3-minute discussion period. Each person or team argues for their way during that

interval. Then vote again. Record your score. This variation limits the number of ideas that are argued each round, and gives time to raise points in favour of each.

This last format rewards those who are articulate. One round the vote was 3-1. But the person who voted alone spoke so convincingly that the re-vote was 4-0 in favour of that person's way.

Conclusion

This game stimulated fervent debate. Players have strong feelings about feminist issues. The ranking of policies in the game coincides with an issue in the feminist movement: Where should feminists put their efforts first?

When we direct players to figure out what the most popular policy would be, some respond, "Who care what benighted ideas other people have? I am only concerned with being a true feminist."

Hopefully, the game will draw participants' attention to the variety of reasonable courses of action that will contribute to women's equality.

Reprinted from SIMULATION/GAMING/NEWS, September 1975. Used by permission of the author.

A glass bead game

Adapted from Herman Hesse's *Magister Ludi or The Glass Bead Game* by Kennith A. Smith

Herman Hesse's novel describes a sophisticated game played by secularised monks of the future. This glass bead game is designed to foster intellectual growth and a mystical understanding of the basic unity of the universe by putting players in a position in which they connect different ideas and items in the universe through mental bridges. Below is an adaptation of the glass bead game for adult use.

1. Divide the group into pairs or two teams.

2. Give each member of a pair or each team a supply of "glass beads" (paper slips cut in the shape of a circle) and a marking pen.

3. Seat the members of the pair or the two teams opposite each other.

4. Appoint a judge and recorder.

5. Have each side write down an idea or thought or name on one circle.

6. Begin the game by having one side reveal its idea, concept etc.

7. Have the other side then reveal its idea or "glass bead".

8. The first side must then mentally connect the two different ideas within two minutes.

9. If it fails, the other side is given one point, and the failing side then writes another "bead" and gives the opponent the two minute challenge of connecting the new "bead" with the last idea connected. If it succeeds, it then writes another bead and returns the challenge of connecting this new bead to the chain.

10. The game continues until the agreed upon limit has been reached.

11. The side with the most points wins.

12. Debrief by examining the chain constructed, checking the most difficult concepts to connect, patterns of thought which have been revealed, areas in which knowledge is limited, and "super-beads", i.e. long chains which seem to go in circles.

Adaptations and variations:

1. Try the glass bead game limiting the subject area to a particular discipline such as biology, religion or music.

2. Try wide open glass bead games with no limits.

3. Allow either negative or positive connectives or both.

4. Use the connective developed as the automatic second bead.

5. Limit the eligible beads to a pre-developed vocabulary list.

6. Pre-select the concepts, write them on the beads before the game, shuffle the beads, and deal them to the opponents.

Reprinted from SIMULATION SHARING SERVICE, October 1976. Used by permission.

An example of a glass bead chain played by a team of adults:

Bead 1	Bead 2	Connective
evolution	Jesus	Teilhard de Chardin
Jesus	war	"wars and rumours of wars"
war	Emily Post	Geneva Convention
Emily Post	Hebrew grammar	correct form
Hebrew grammar	women's lib	neuter gender
women's lib	Christmas eve	"and on earth, peace, good will to people"

Making and improving

A game that dramatises some basic economic concepts

Purpose

To provide an opportunity for participants to experience non-verbally some basic economic concepts such as "raw material", "investment", "capital", "manufactured goods", currency", "division of labour", "value added", etc. The activity also provides practice in quick decision-making, in discussion skills, and in seeing a problem as a whole rather than in fragments. It is enjoyable, and hence contributes to motivation. In a more elaborate form it dramatises some important aspects of world trade.

Preparation

It is necessary to have some pencils; some sheets of ordinary white paper; some sheets of sticky coloured paper; some pairs of scissors; and a stock of home-made paper money.

The leader also needs to prepare in advance four types of template, made out of stiff card. The four outlines for these templates are: a saloon car; a television set; a television screen; a star. You need as many copies of each template as there are groups taking part in the activity. (Hence at least two copies of each template.) The template for the car should be roughly twice the area of the template for the TV set.

Procedure

At its simplest, this activity is no more, so to speak, than an enjoyable game. It could be played at a party, for example, and people would enjoy it without noticing or caring that it dramatises some basic economic concepts. The procedure is as follows.

1. There are two or more teams. A team could at a pinch be a single individual. Better, it is a group of four or five. There is also a "market place", which needs to be represented by at least two people.

2. Each team is given 20 units of currency in paper money, a buying list, a selling list, and a set of rules. The lists and rules should be explained and discussed before starting, so that they are entirely clear.

3. The buying list is this:
Templates cost 4 units each.
Scissors and pencils cost 3 units each.
Sheets of sticky coloured paper cost 2 units each.
Sheets of ordinary white paper cost 1 unit each.

4. The selling list is this:
A television set cut out of white paper is worth 1 unit.
A white television set with a coloured screen is worth 2 units.
A car cut out of white paper is worth 3 units.
A white car with a coloured star on its bonnet is worth 4 units.

5. The rules are these:

a)   There is first a discussion time of 5 minutes during which each team can decide what it's going to do.

b) There is then 15 minutes during which the teams can buy and make and sell. All buying is from the market place and all selling is to it, at the prices stated above.

c) At the end of 15 minutes the winning team is the one which has the most "wealth". This will be worked out from the prices stated above.

d) It would of course be cheating to use paper or pencils other than those bought from the market place.

Discussion

There is much to discuss and to follow up. These are some of the main questions which the leader may wish in particular to raise and explore:

- What were the methods employed by the winning team? Did they win through good luck, or through good management? Either way, how did they make the decision they did? Did they behave in ways which other teams would describe as selfish or unfair?

- How did participants feel about the jobs they found themselves doing? What were the most interesting and enjoyable jobs? Did everyone actually have a job? Or were there, so to speak, "pockets of unemployment"? Were there some "human resources" being wasted? How did the people concerned feel about this?

- What aspects of the real world were dramatised? For example, what is the meaning of terms such as "capital", "investment", "raw material", "mass production", "manufactured goods"? What, in the real world, do the templates and scissors represent?

- A fundamental activity of human beings is to take raw things out of the planet, and to process them in some way, and to consume them. But who decides what should be taken out ("extracted")? And how it should be processed? And who should consume it? What are the different ways in which different societies have arranged these matters? What are the main ways in which, actually in history, human beings have found raw materials, and bought, borrowed, begged or stolen raw materials?

- What conflicts and feelings are there in the real world corresponding to the conflicts and feelings expressed in this game?

Reprinted from LEARNING FOR CHANGE IN WORLD SOCIETY (London: World Studies Project, 1976)

Tamuse

A game about cooperation by Gillian Feest

Aim

To experience (or observe) how a group can cooperate non-verbally to solve a puzzle.

Procedure

1. Two sets of eight (large) cards numbered one to eight are needed.

2. One set is laid out on the floor in the arrangement given below as the solution.

3. Eight people are asked to stand one beside each card.

4. They are each given their starting position card to hold. That is, the person standing by Card 1 is given starting position Card 2, the person standing by Card 2 is given starting position Card 4 and so on. (Move the person in the centre to the bottom right hand corner.)

5. The task is for the eight to rearrange themselves so that the person holding Card 1 is standing on the space marked with Card 1, the person holding Card 2 is standing on the space marked with Card 2, etc.

6. There are five rules:
   (a) No talking
   (b) No diagonal moves
   (c) Only one person on each square at any time
   (d) No exchange of cards
   (e) Only one person moving at a time.

The rest of the group can observe or there can be more than one group doing the task and the element of competition be explored.

Questions that can be used afterwards:

1. How did the group arrive at decisions to move?

2. What non-verbal signs were used?

3. Was there frustration because
   (a) someone could not move?
   (b) someone was being pushed around?
   (c) someone was ignored?

4. What other feelings did people have?

5. What did you learn about working in a group?

Starting position

2	4	6
5		8
3	1	7

Solution

1	2	3
4	5	6
7	8	

Reprinted from VALUES by permission of Wheaton Publishers Limited.

Culture game

A game to show misunderstandings that can occur between cultures

Procedure

1. Have discussion on what a culture is, and the importance or not of customs. List points on blackboard or overhead projector.

2. Then divide into three groups, A, B and C. A and B find an area apart from other groups and attempt to work out the culture and customs of their own tribe by –

a)   devloping a basic language (gestures etc.)

b)   type of greeting and farewell (touch or not)

c)   eating habits (utensils – type or not)

d)   a form of entertainment

e)   rule of individuals in tribe.

3. Group C merely divides into two observation groups and observes the preparations.

4. When culture is developed, tribe A comes to tribe B's village for a meeting to discuss how they can live together.

5. Group C observes both groups in their preparation and in meeting and makes notes:

a)   Did they convert to known language and gestures?

b)   What were difficulties of communication?

c)   How did some of the customs develop – through need etc?

d)   What were difficulties in organising?

6. Have a group discussion on the things that group C had to observe.

Note:
(1) Groups may need help to get started.
(2) When the two groups do come together, there may be a great deal of difficulty and frustration. Groups must work out their own problems.

Time: 90 minutes.

Variations

1. Group C can prepare tribal customs and the three groups meet.

2. Change groups so that a different group observes.

Discussion

1. People from different countries are often called by nicknames, e.g. wogs, polacks, krauts etc. What is the reason for this? Discuss.

2. Discuss what changes people from other countries have made to your community in terms of clothing, housing, food, transport etc.

3. Discuss the different customs of different countries, e.g. Christmas, greetings, marriage. How did these develop differently? Why do we sometimes laugh at customs different from our own? What can we do to overcome prejudice?

4. Discuss the similarity of languages and customs of different countries.

5. Find out in how many languages you can say "hello".

Reprinted from PEOPLE INTERACTING, Sturt CAE (Adelaide), 1978. Used by permission.

Nuclear Negotiations

A simulation by Darryl Grafton

Objective:

The object of this simulation game is to make participants aware of the difficulties of cooperation between countries with different histories. It also attempts to make participants aware of the real difficulties of political and nuclear arms negotiations between countries. After the game, participants should have an awareness of these difficulties and be able to express them with clarity.

The game deals with issues of cooperation and what it means to be open to different views and opinions. This game goes well with a Bible study on nuclear war, or war in general.

Running time: 60-80 minutes for the game itself and 20-30 minutes for debriefing and discussion.

Materials needed: statistical information on the countries (included), background histories of each country (included), a map of the world Continent (included), and a large playing area.

The space or layout of the game is important. Participants need enough room to move around in, as there will probably be a lot of talking and walking. A small room will get significantly hotter because of the amount of talking and moving the participants will do within the hour. Each country should have a base of operations that they can return to for discussion. It is recommended that each country have a separate room in which to meet. If a large, single room is used, then countries should be spaced far apart. Some type of markers (flags, lines, signs) should be made to designate country territory.

Number of participants: 6 to 24 people plus the game director. If necessary the country of Messer may be represented by the game director. Participants should be divided more or less evenly between the three or four countries to be represented, with a maximum of 6 to a country. If

the group is larger than 24, it is better to run two separate simulations, each with a game director.

Scenario : This game takes place on a world called "Continent". The four countries of Continent have varying histories and nuclear capabilities. A dispute has arisen which needs to be settled. Participants may negotiate with representatives of the other countries in any way they wish. The outcome of the simulation is entirely dependent on the decisions of the participants.

Representatives of each country will receive
1) a map of Continent

2) a statistical layout for all the countries of Continent

3) the background history of their own country **for their eyes only.**

As the game begins, Messer, the smallest country of Continent, has been attacked by a small force in an attempted invasion. The other countries blame one another for the attack. Negotiations take place according to the will of the participants.

Notes for the game director

This game involves four different countries: Messer, Ul-Marion, West Durkur and Turgon. Each country has its own version of the history of Continent, with a strong bias towards itself as the righteous nation. None of the four countries sees itself at fault in any way. Hence none of the "histories" are completely truthful. Each country takes a subjective view of what has gone before and of the relationships between the countries of Continent. There is no real way to discover the actual truth of the situation. If the game is to be ended with full cooperation between countries, participants must learn to accept the differences and deal with them, rather than force others to submit to their will.

Your purpose as game director is to cause as much controversy as possible! This may be done by bringing out the differences in the understanding of events. For instance, Ul-Marion does not believe it has invaded Messer, yet Messer claims it can prove that Ul-Marion was the invader. You may move from group to group, encouraging distrust of the other countries.

Announce the time limit (60-80 minutes) before the game begins. After the countries gather to announce their final actions (which may lead to a sudden call to launch nuclear weapons), the participants should take a break before debriefing. Participants should not sit in their respective countries during the debriefing and discussion.

General information

(to be read to participants):

Each of you belongs to a country in the world called "Continent". Each country will receive a copy of its own history, together with a statistical sheet containing information on all the major countries, including nuclear capabilities.

Several days ago, Messer was attacked by a small, unidentified invading force. The attack was unsuccessful. The World Council of Continent has called an emergency meeting. Called to the meeting are representatives of Messer, Ul-Marion, West Durkur and Turgon (at Messer's request).

The object of the game is to settle the dispute. You may speak and negotiate with any country you wish. You may also choose not to speak or negotiate with any country. You may sign pacts if you choose. You may use any or all of your nuclear weapons whenever you wish. **Any action you wish to take must be reported to the game director before it is carried out.** At the end of the negotiations, the meeting of the Council will be called, and you must state your final action to the Council.

Here are some suggestions to help you in the game:

1. Study your country's history carefully.

2. Talk – or do not talk – to other countries as you choose.

3. Sign written peace pacts with any country.

4. Make verbal peace pacts with any country.

5. You may lie or tell the truth.

6. You may fire all or some of your nuclear weapons whenever you wish.

7. Any action you intend to take should be reported to the game director before you actually do it.

Questions for debriefing and discussion

1. What was most frustrating abou the negotiations?

2. How could some of the frustration have been avoided?

3. Do you think that real countries experience this type of frustration? How might they overcome it?

4. What do you feel really happened? After the answers to this question have been given, explain that each country's history was written from a biased and subjective point of view, and that the truth of the story could never have been discovered.

5. Do you think, in real life, that there is any one country (including your own country) that is ever 100% correct in its assessment of history? Why?/Why not?

6. Is there anything you did not feel good about during the game? What was it?

7. Was there any action in the game that was a "Christian" action? What was it?

8. If you could play the game over again, what would you do differently? Why?

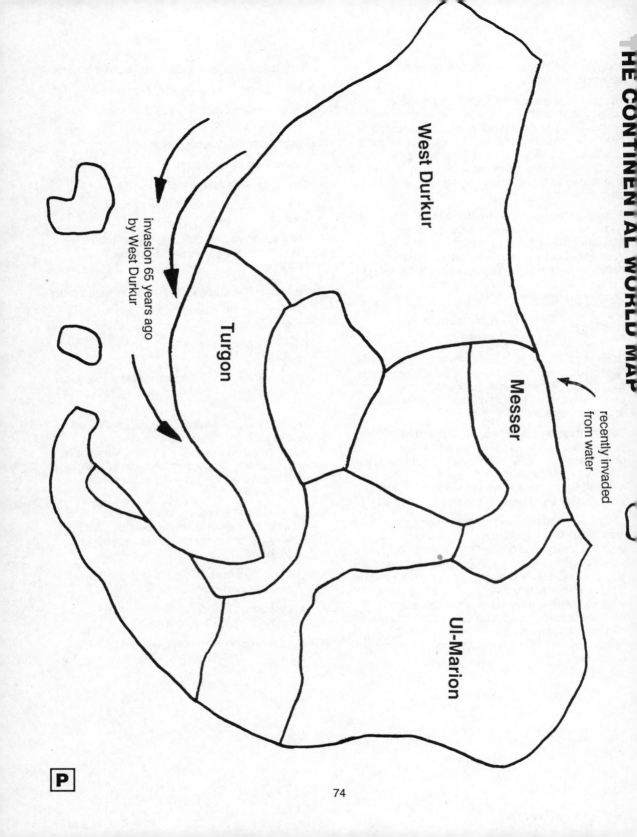

West Durkur

Turgon

invasion 65 years ago
by West Durkur

Messer

recently invaded
from water

Ul-Marion

P

Statistical information

Notes:

The **food distribution** percentage is the number of people out of one hundred who are able to eat a balanced diet. For instance, a 65% rating means that 65 people out of every hundred are able to eat a proper meal each day. Ul-Marion has enough food so that everyone in the country is able to eat four times as much food per day as they actually need.

The **nuclear attack/defence** percentage is the amount of weaponry held by that country. If a country decides to attack another country, they choose what percentage of their attack capability they will use. If a country is attacked by another country, it is assumed that they will use their entire defensive capability. The formula for an attack is as follows:

Attack percentage of the aggressor
– defence percentage or the country attacked
= percentage of damage to the country under attack.

If a country is damaged 100% it is considered utterly devastated and defeated and can take no further part in the simulation.

Ul-Marion

Population:	350 million
Government:	presidential democracy
Economy:	excellent
Production:	poor
Food distribution:	400%
Nuclear attack:	65%
Nuclear defence:	35%

West Durkur

Population:	200 million
Government:	dictatorship
Economy:	good
Production:	fair
Food distribution:	75%
Nuclear attack:	85%
Nuclear defence:	15%

Turgon

Population:	75 million
Government:	parliamentary democracy
Economy:	poor
Production:	poor
Food distribution:	55%
Nuclear attack:	10%
Nuclear defence:	90%

Messer

Population:	20 million
Government:	socialist
Economy:	fair
Production:	fair
Food distribution:	70%
Nuclear attack:	35%
Nuclear defence:	nil

History of Ul-Marion

(for Ul-Marion citizens only!)

Ul-Marion has been the leading country of Continent for over 200 years. Our wealth and production have led the world and have become an example of the good life. We have had the most stable economy and production on Continent.

Over the past twenty years, however, the economy has been faltering. The slow process of a democracy is finally catching up with us. Despite this setback, we are convinced that Ul-Marion holds the best government because it is government for the people – it allows all the people to take part in the decision making processes.

Many other countries have been jealous of the power and wealth which has come as a result of our hard work. Thus we have been attacked politically for some time. West Durkur, especially, has been at odds with us, claiming that we are attempting to take over the world. This is simply not true. We are definitely opposed to West Durkur's form of government and foreign policies. Sixty-five years ago West Durkur invaded a neighbouring country, Turgon, and only pulled out on our orders ten years later. Trouble has been brewing for some time and we foresee some type of unavoidable confrontation developing.

Several days ago, our small neighbour, Messer, was attacked from the sea. The attack was unsuccessful. West Durkur has pointed the finger at us, claiming that we attempted to invade Messer. This is clearly an excuse for West Durkur to form an alliance with Turgon in mounting a possible nuclear attack. Our sources indicate that it was, in fact, a West Durkurn force that attacked Messer.

History of West Durkur

(for West Durkurn citizens only!)

Our country definitely has the most efficient form of government on Continent: a dictatorship. Our great leader orders the task and it is immediately done. This is not even comparable to the slow process of a democracy which Ul-Marion has. In the past, Ul-Marion has been the leading country economically. They have been very smug and self-righteous when it comes to their way of life, and are a very selfish country. But the flaws in their style of government are finally catching up with them, and their economy is faltering. Our country is now moving to the forefront in the economic world, and Ul-Marion is definitely jealous of our advances.

Sixty-five years ago Turgon, our south-eastern neighbour, was undergoing an economic collapse, and our great leader of the time offered help. When Turgon refused, our leader decided to help anyway. Our forces moved in and established a new economic order which was for the benefit of the country. Ten years later, when the economy of Turgon was stable, we pulled out, just as our leader had promised. However, Turgon does not seem to trust us any more.

Several days ago the small northern country of Messer was attacked, and our sources have identified Ul-Marion as the aggressor. This is obviously a last ditch effort by Ul-Marion to take over the whole of Continent and save its failing economy. Ul-Marion denies this and actually claims that *we* attacked Messer. Furthermore, Ul-Marion is attempting to get Turgon on their side.

History of Turgon

(for Turgan citizens only!)

Our country is slowly recovering from an economic depression which occurred some seventy years ago. The recovery, however, was forced on us by West Durkur, who moved in with force and took over our country until the economy was stable. Although West Durkur did stabilise the economy somewhat, they took as "payment" an unreasonable amount of exports during their ten-year occupation. We do not trust them. Our relationship with Ul-Marion is not very good either.

Ul-Marion likes to appear friendly, but they refuse to share their abundance of food with us. We do as little business as possible with this selfish country.

Recently Messer, a small country on the northern shores of Continent, was attacked from the sea. Messer has sent secret envoys to us, claiming that it was Ul-Marion who attempted the invasion. Trouble is brewing on Continent. We must side with someone or we will not survive the coming war.

History of Messer

(for Messern citizens only!)

Our country is small and insignificant by comparison with our neighbours. Many larger countries have attempted to usurp our land through non-military means – particularly West Durkur and Ul-Marion – but we have refused to submit either to West Durkur's aggressive posturing or to Ul-Marion's selfish attitudes.

A few days ago there was an attempted invasion of our country. This has caused concern throughout Continent. Our sources indicate that the attackers came from Ul-Marion. (Ul-Marion has been trying to get us to merge with them for the past forty years. We have strenuously resisted, not only because of that country's selfishness, but also because we can see that their economy is failing.) We are not surprised that finally they have resorted to the use

of force. Ul-Marion (naturally) denies all responsibility for the attack on our shores.

We were approached by the Turgan ambassador, asking for information on the attack, and we told him what we knew – that Ul-Marion had attempted to invade us and had been repelled. Ul-Marion continues to deny that they were responsible, but we know they are lying. We are in a delicate situation. If we say openly that we have been attacked by Ul-Marion, there is a strong possibility that Ul-Marion will move against us again with full force: an attack which we might not survive. So we must move cautiously, acting as though we do not know who was responsible for the attempted invasion.

The structural violence game

A game by Vanessa Lynne designed to provide participants with first-hand experience of the complicated concept of structural violence

Objective

To explore the concept of "structural violence" through role play.

Props

ball of string or wool
packet of chocolate coated biscuits
packet of plain dry crackers
2 icecream containers to store the biscuits
computer paper for wall charts
four only felt-tipped pens
pile of scrap paper for folding and decorating
wall charts of "rules" and "scenario"
list of "private rules"
yellow and green sticky spots – ratio of 2:1
Blutak

Preparation

A large open space is best. In a classroom it is best to clear desks and chairs. Section off a corner of the room with the string and make it just large enough for two-thirds of the group to fit in with standing room only.

Scenario (reproduce on a wall chart)

Yellow and Green are neighbouring countries.

Green supplies Yellow with paper to fold and decorate with pens (which are found only in the Yellow country).

Green buys the finished product and pays in biscuits.

Yellow depends on this industry in order to survive.

Green sell the finished product to the Green food distributor who pays his/her fellow Greens in chocolate biscuits.

Green's life style and status is measured by the quality and quantity of the folded paper. Payment is calculated by quality and quantity.

Rules (reproduce on a wall chart)

Yellows may not leave their country.

Greens may come and go as they please.

Yellows may not talk to Greens or to more than one Yellow at a time.

Greens have no restriction on their freedom of speech.

Yellows may use paper and pens.

Green police enforce these rules.

PRIVATE RULES (reproduce on a small sheet of paper for the Greens only to see)

Unless the paper is folded and decorated satisfactorily, Green will not supply Yellow with food.

Maximum payment is one biscuit per piece of paper.

Payment may be withheld if the workers are heard to complain.

Payment is actually in crackers, not in chocolate biscuits.

Playing the game

1. Sit the participants in a circle to explain the rules of the game.

2. Distribute the spots (two yellow for every one green) separating friends where possible and making sure that the Greens are not all one sex in a mixed group. Have everyone stick their spot on their forehead.

3. Display wall charts and allow a few minutes for questions.

4. Send Yellows to the sectioned-off corner of the room.

5. Give the containers of biscuits to one of the Greens whose job it now is to distribute them.

6. Give one chocolate biscuit to one of the Yellows to share with the whole of the rest of the Yellow group and indicate that this is being done in the interests of fairness!

7. Make sure that the Greens do not declare that the other container holds crackers.

8. Appoint one or more Greens to be police or allow the Greens to decide.

9. Give the Yellows the felt tipped pens, and the paper to the Greens who will give it to the Yellows once the game starts.

10. Hand the "Private Rules" to one of the Greens.

11. Allow 3-5 minutes for people to get into their roles.

12. Start the game. There is no set time for the running of this game. Much depends on the group. Fifteen minutes is a workable time. Some groups get very involved and time should be allowed for them to keep going. Other groups get disillusioned very quickly and the attention of some participants may wander. It is best to stop the game after the fifteen minutes if this is the case.

13. When time is up, call everyone to sit in a circle.

14. Each participant in turn should now have the opportunity to state how they feel about their role. Individuals may "pass" if they wish. This time is for sharing, not for discussing.

Evaluation

Time should now be made available for discussion.

Discussion starters such as the following may be used:

- What happened?
- How many forms of structural violence were observed?
- What did the Yellow group do? How did they react?
- What did the Green group do? How did they react?
- What positive steps could both parties have taken to improve the situation?
- Why did the Yellows allow themselves to be oppressed?
- What are parallel situations in the world that were reflected in this game?
- What do the two types of biscuits represent?

Conclusion

Ask all of the participants to remove their coloured spots. Share out the biscuits amongst the Yellows if there are any left.

Explanation

Because structural violence is such a difficult concept to grasp it could be treated in a way other than the traditional "chalk and talk" method. The STRUCTURAL VIOLENCE GAME is one such method.

However, it should be remembered that simulations oversimplify and mask the complex and deep rooted nature of structural violence. Participants will need to be guided towards an understanding of these complexities.

Since the inception of the game during the last half of 1984, it has been changed and modified on a number of occasions. The original version appeared in PEACEMEAL Vol 1 No 3. In this version the "oppressed" section of the class rolled newspapers to "sell" to their "oppressors" but the temptation to use them as weapons proved irresistable on a number of occasions. A potentially less violent version is printed here.

The evaluation session, particularly after "violence" has broken out, is most revealing. Young people are very quickly able to see how oppression can lead to revolution.

There are some interesting observations to be made about the circumstances under which the newspapers were used as weapons. Older participants were far more restrained, using threats rather than actions. On the other hand, a class of Year 9 students took no time at all to discover the alternative use for the newspapers and seemed to thoroughly enjoy the experience.

The question of oppression and revolution may still be adequately covered using the "softer" version of the game. During the evaluation session with a mixed group of Years 9 and 11 I asked what would have happened if the "oppressed" had been allowed to have a cricket bat as well as the paper and pens. Many of the group said that they would have used it.

Another very revealing question to ask is "If we were to play the game over again now and the roles were reversed, how would you react in your new role?" In my experience the response is almost always "I'd be worse" from the formerly "oppressed" group.

Having facilitated the game on numerous occasions, I have never ceased to be amazed at the range of strategies people use in order to procure a chocolate biscuit. In their simulated form I have seen the "oppressed" try coercion, blackmail, selling-out their fellow sufferers, bartering, striking, sabotage and subterfuge. The "oppressors" use stand-over tactics, threats, introduce "*agents provocateurs*", withdraw the raw materials, flaunt chocolate biscuits in front of the "oppressed", make deals, bribe and cheat. In a number of cases the "oppressed" have felt so disillusioned that they have stretched out on the floor and "died". A proportion of the "oppressors" in every game feel dreadful about what they are doing and either withdraw from the playing of the game or try to make the conditions of the "oppressed" a little better – the social change activists of the future perhaps? Leaders of the "oppressed" usually emerge too, with well orchestrated strikes and boycotts being organised.

On the occasions when teachers have joined in the game I have made sure that they join the ranks of the "oppressed". In this role they are far less likely to take over and try to direct proceedings. Many teachers have indicated that they felt powerless: squeezed in with the others, unable to be in control, and with their freedom of movement and speech curtailed.

The game is a valuable teaching aid, but not the whole story in dealing with the issues and concepts of structural violence. To be of any value at all, preparation, evaluation and follow-up are essential.

Your own personal evaluation of the game would be most welcome to assist with the further development of this game and others to follow. Please send any comments to:
Vanessa Lynne, *Solutions* (Conflict Resolution Services), PO Box 1337, Fremantle, Western Australia 6160.

Reprinted from EDUCATING FOR PEACE JUSTICE AND HOPE, Vanessa Letham, ed., 1986. Used by permission of the author.